# Use It! Don't Lose It!

# MATH
## Daily Skills Practice
## Grade 8

by Marjorie Frank

**Incentive**Publications

*Illustrated by Kathleen Bullock*
*Cover by Geoffrey Brittingham*
*Edited by Jill Norris*
*Copyedited by Cary Grayson and Steve Carlon*

ISBN 978-0-86530-667-7

8   9   10        13   12

*Printed by Sheridan Books, Inc., Chelsea, Michigan • January 2012*
www.incentivepublications.com

# Don't let those math skills get lost or rusty!

As a teacher you work hard to teach math skills to your students. Your students work hard to master them. Do you worry that your students will forget the material as you move on to the next concept?

If so, here's a plan for you and your students—one that will keep those skills sharp.

**Use It! Don't Lose It!** provides daily math practice for all the basic skills. There are five math problems a day, every day for 36 weeks. The skills are correlated to national and state standards.

Students practice all the eighth grade skills, concepts, and processes in a spiraling sequence. The plan starts with the simplest level of eighth grade skills, progressing gradually to higher-level tasks, as it continually circles around and back to the the same skills at a little higher level, again and again. Each time a skill shows up, it has a new context—requiring students to dig into their memories, recall what they know, and apply it to another situation.

## The Weekly Plan—Five Problems a Day for 36 Weeks

**Monday – Thursday** .............. • one computation item
  Monday – whole numbers    Wednesday – integers
  Tuesday – decimals    Thursday – fractions
• one problem-solving task (word problem)
• one algebra item

**Monday** and **Wednesday** ....... • one statistics or probability item
• one geometry item

**Tuesday** and **Thursday** .......... • one measurement item
• one number concepts item

**Friday**.................................... • two computation items
• one algebra item
• one item rotating among math strands
• one *Challenge Problem* demanding more involved steps, thinking skills, and calculations (making use of several skills)

## Contents

# How to Use Daily Skills Practice

To get started, reproduce each page, slice the Monday–Thursday lesson pages in half or prepare a transparency. The lessons can be used . . .

- **for independent practice**—Reproduce the lessons and let students work individually or in pairs to practice skills at the beginning or end of a math class.
- **for small group work**—Students can discuss and solve the problems together and agree on answers.
- **for the whole class review**—Make a transparency and work through the problems together as a class.

## Helpful Hints for Getting Started

- Though students may work alone on the items, always find a way to review and discuss the answers together. In each review, ask students to describe how they solved the problem-solving problems or other problems that involve choices of strategies.

- Allow more time for the Friday lesson. The Challenge Problem may take a little longer. Students can work in small groups to discover good strategies and correct answers for this problem.

- Provide measurement tools and other supplies students need for solving the problems. There will not be room on the sheet for all problems to be solved. Students will need scratch paper for their work.

- Decide ahead of time about the use of calculators. Since the emphasis is on students practicing their skills, it is recommended that the items be done without calculators and other calculation aids. If you want to focus specifically on technology skills, set a particular goal for certain lessons to be done or checked with calculators. You might allow calculator use for the Friday Challenge Problems.

- The daily lessons are designed to be completed in a short time period, so that they can be used along with your regular daily instruction. However, don't end the discussion until you are sure all students "get it," or at least until you know which ones don't get something and will need extra instruction. This will strengthen all the other work students do in math class.

- Keep a consistent focus on the strategies and processes for problem solving. Encourage students to explore and share different approaches for solving the problems. Explaining (orally or in writing) their problem-solving process is an important math skill. Be open to answers (correct ones, of course) that are not supplied in the Answer Key.

- Take note of which items leave some or all of the students confused or uncertain. This will alert you to which skills need more instruction.

- The daily lessons may include some topics or skills your students have not yet learned. In these cases, students may skip items. Or, you might encourage them to consider how the problem could be solved. Or, you might use the occasion for a short lesson that would get them started on this skill.

**1.** Which sum is larger?

   a.   9,821    (b.)   7,388
        + 7,433        + 9,872
        17 254      17 260

**2.** Can this problem be solved?

A baseball player hit two home runs in the first three games of the season. How many home runs did he hit in the whole season?  No

**3.** Finish the number pattern.

250   245   235   220   _200_   _195_

**4.** In a set of data, the difference between the greatest and least numbers is called the

_____ _range_ _____

**5.** Which pairs of lines are **perpendicular**?

A           B

(C)          D

E          F

When it comes to math, I draw the line.

**1.** Which statement is **not** true?

   (a.) All numbers are natural numbers.
   b. Fractions are rational numbers.
   c. Zero is an integer.

**2.** Write this number in standard notation:

**four hundred thousand four hundred four**

$4 + 100 + 1000 + 4 + 100 + 4$

**3.** Compute:

**90.07 + 0.063 =** $90.133$

**4.** Which of these units of measurement are U.S. customary units?

   (liters)   (inches)   miles   ounces
   pints   (grams)   quarts   (meters)

How do you measure up?

**5.** What information is **not** needed to solve this problem?

Twenty-five percent of the players on the basketball team are taller than Charlie. ~~Half of the players forgot to wash their uniforms.~~ Charlie is 6 feet, 2 inches tall. There are 20 members on the team. How many players are taller than Charlie?

*Name*

1/30/13

**1.** What operation is needed to solve the problem?

The Comets' goalie stopped an average of 45 goal attempts each game. How many goals did he stop in five games? _division_

**2.**

This angle is a(n) _obtuse_ angle.

**3.** What number is the opposite of **55.7**?

−55.7

**4.** Compute: **−12 + 17 =** 5

**5.** During which year did attendance change the most from Game 1 to Game 8? 2003

| Comets Soccer Games Attendance, 2003-2005 | | | |
|---|---|---|---|
| **Game** | **2003** | **2004** | **2005** |
| 1 | 88 | 62 | 99 |
| 2 | 65 | 67 | 75 |
| 3 | 70 | 74 | 80 |
| 4 | 52 | 85 | 90 |
| 5 | 73 | 92 | 115 |
| 6 | 66 | 111 | 142 |
| 7 | 83 | 106 | 130 |
| 8 | 69 | 120 | 150 |

*Name*

1/31/13

**1.** What is the absolute value of **−50**?

50

**2.** Compute: $\frac{3}{12} + \frac{1}{12} + \frac{7}{12} =$ $\frac{11}{12}$

**3.** Put these in order from least to greatest:

**3,333; 30,303; 3,003; 33,033; 3,033**

3003; 3033; 3333; 30303; 33033

**4.** At a tennis tournament, 96 players drank a total of 768 liters of water. On the average, how many liters did each player drink?

8 liters

96 )768
   768
    /0

**5.** Measure the picture of the tennis racquet in centimeters.
(Round to the nearest half centimeter.)
8.4

Measure it in inches.
(Round to the nearest half inch.)
3.5

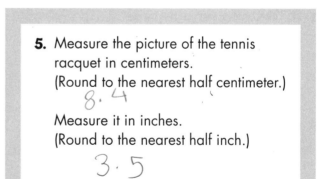
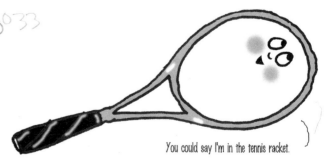

You could say I'm in the tennis racket.

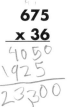

*Name* Naivalya Tallan

2/1/13

**1.** Compute:    $- 19 - 63 =$ -82

**2.** Compute:    675
         x 36

4050
1925
23300

You can count on me.

**3.** Which expression matches the words?

**the difference between nine times a number and thirty**

   a. 30n – 9     b. (30 – 9) n    c. 9n – 30     d. n + 30 – 9

**4.** Which event has the **least** likelihood of happening?

     a. The sun will come up tomorrow.
     b. If you reach into a bag with ten red socks and three white socks, you will grab a white sock.
     c. If you toss one die, you will get a five.
     d. Fall will come right after spring.

# 5. Challenge Problem

At the end of a football game, five players gathered in a group to congratulate each other. Each player slapped the back of each other player. How many backslaps were there? The diagram can help you figure it out.

20 back slaps

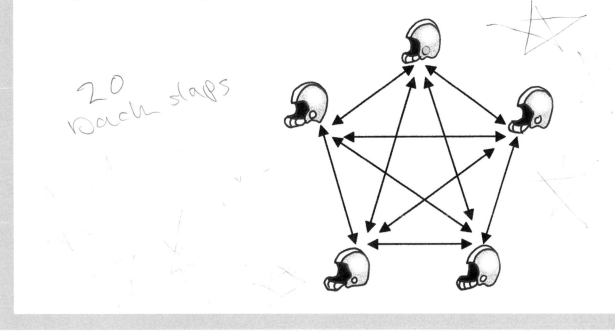

*Name*

2/5/13

**1.** Which expression matches the words?

**the sum of fifteen and six times the square of a number (n)**

a. $15 + 62$
b. $6n + 152$
c. $15 + 6n^2$  *(circled)*

**2.** Compute:   **12946**
                **− 3789**
                    9157

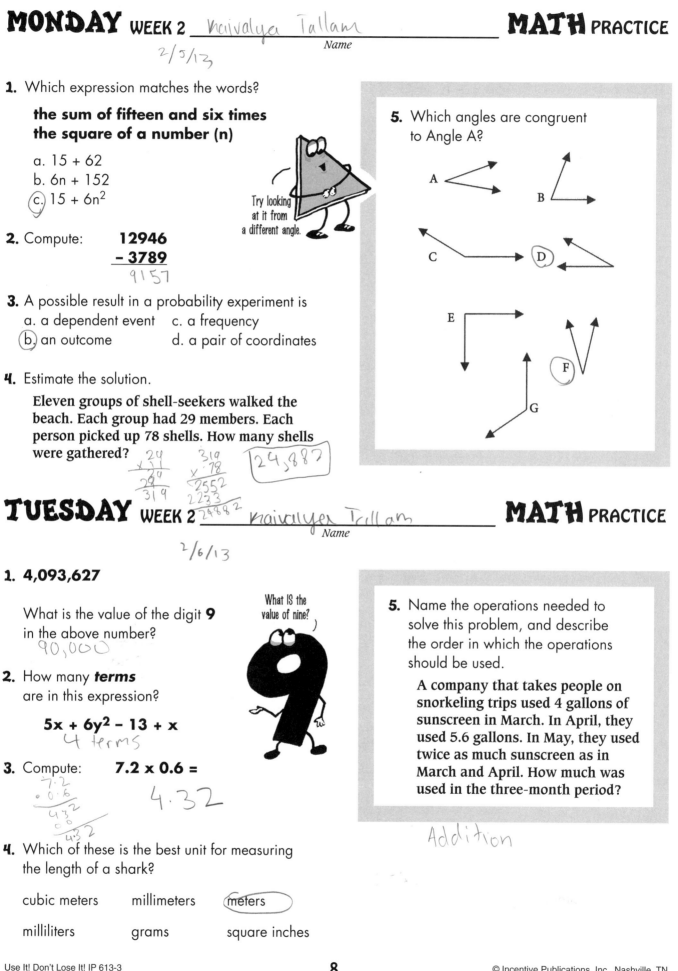

Try looking at it from a different angle.

**3.** A possible result in a probability experiment is
a. a dependent event    c. a frequency
b. an outcome  *(circled)*    d. a pair of coordinates

**4.** Estimate the solution.

Eleven groups of shell-seekers walked the beach. Each group had 29 members. Each person picked up 78 shells. How many shells were gathered?

24
x 11
24
319

319
x 78
2552
2233
24882

24,882

**5.** Which angles are congruent to Angle A?

A    B
C    D
E    F
G

*Name*

2/6/13

**1.** **4,093,627**

What is the value of the digit **9** in the above number?
90,000

What IS the value of nine?

**2.** How many **terms** are in this expression?

$$5x + 6y^2 - 13 + x$$

4 terms

**3.** Compute:   **7.2 x 0.6 =**
7.2
0.6
432
00
4.32

4.32

**4.** Which of these is the best unit for measuring the length of a shark?

cubic meters    millimeters    meters *(circled)*

milliliters    grams    square inches

**5.** Name the operations needed to solve this problem, and describe the order in which the operations should be used.

A company that takes people on snorkeling trips used 4 gallons of sunscreen in March. In April, they used 5.6 gallons. In May, they used twice as much sunscreen as in March and April. How much was used in the three-month period?

Addition

# WEDNESDAY WEEK 2 _____Kaivalya Tallam_____ MATH PRACTICE

1. The world's longest beach towel is 14.46 meters long. An ordinary beach towel measures 1.62 meters. What is the difference in their lengths?

$$14.46$$
$$- 1.62$$
$$\overline{12.84}$$

*Don't throw in the towel.*

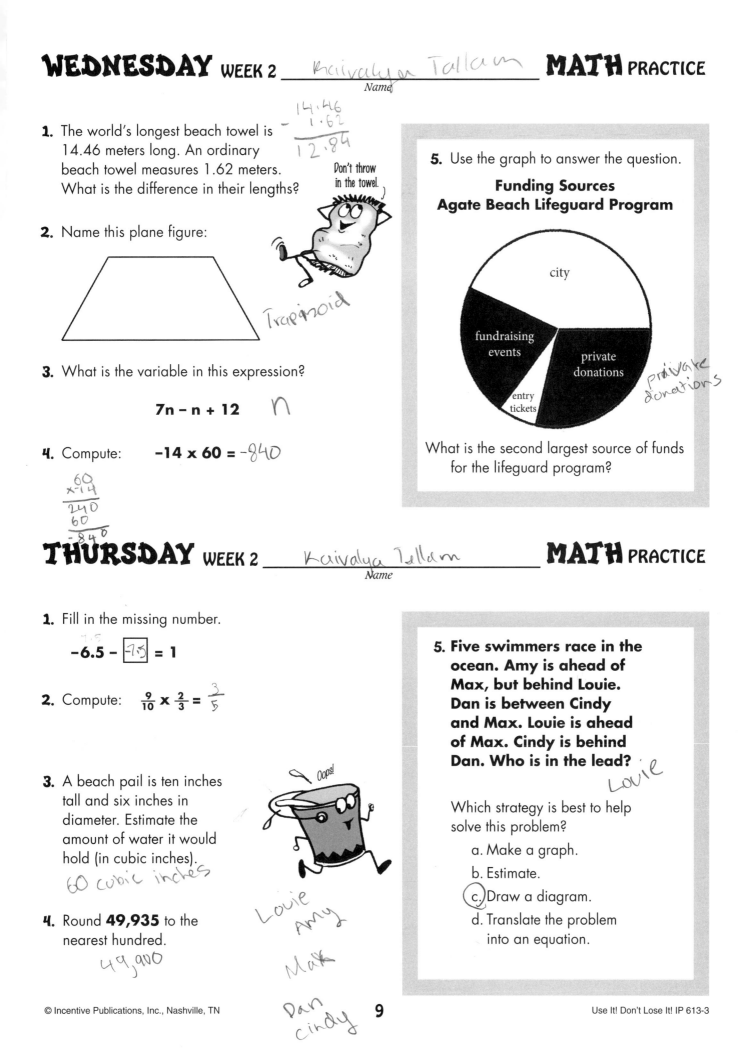

2. Name this plane figure:

Trapezoid

3. What is the variable in this expression?

$$7n - n + 12$$    $n$

4. Compute:    $-14 \times 60 =$ $-840$

$$60$$
$$\times 14$$
$$\overline{240}$$
$$60$$
$$\overline{-840}$$

5. Use the graph to answer the question.

**Funding Sources
Agate Beach Lifeguard Program**

city

fundraising events

private donations    *private donations*

entry tickets

What is the second largest source of funds for the lifeguard program?

# THURSDAY WEEK 2 _____Kaivalya Tallam_____ MATH PRACTICE

1. Fill in the missing number.

$$-6.5 - \boxed{-7.5} = 1$$

2. Compute:    $\dfrac{9}{10} \times \dfrac{2}{3} = \dfrac{3}{5}$

3. A beach pail is ten inches tall and six inches in diameter. Estimate the amount of water it would hold (in cubic inches).

60 cubic inches

*Oops!*

4. Round **49,935** to the nearest hundred.

49,900

5. Five swimmers race in the ocean. Amy is ahead of Max, but behind Louie. Dan is between Cindy and Max. Louie is ahead of Max. Cindy is behind Dan. Who is in the lead?

Louie

Which strategy is best to help solve this problem?
   a. Make a graph.
   b. Estimate.
   c. Draw a diagram.
   d. Translate the problem into an equation.

Louie
Amy
Max
Dan
Cindy

**1.** Compute: $-\frac{1}{3} + \frac{2}{6} + \frac{1}{4} =$

$$\frac{8}{24} + \frac{8}{24} + \frac{6}{24} = \frac{6}{24} = \frac{1}{4}$$

**3.** In the following equation, what is the **coefficient** of the variable?

$$-30y + 4 = 64$$

$-30$

**2.** Which demonstrates the **associative property for addition?**

a. (90 + 4) + 15 = 90 + (4 + 15)

b. 8 x 9 = 9 x 6

c. 77 + 12 = 12 + 77

d. 1,399,000 + 0 = 1,399,000

e. 3 (7 + 9) = (3 x 7) + (3 x 9)

**4.** What is the mean of this set of data?

| 7 min. | 24 min. | 36 min |
|--------|---------|--------|
| 18 min. | 3 min. | 41 min. |
| 20 min. | 18 min. | 22 min. |

90  189
66  153
48  112

$9\overline{)189}$   21

# 5. Challenge Problem

A crab has spent her afternoon crawling around the outside edge of Sam's beach towel. So far, the crab has made six trips around the entire perimeter of the towel without stopping. This crab doesn't like to crawl much more than 500 feet in an afternoon. How many more times will she need to crawl the perimeter in order to reach the total of 500 feet?

24 times

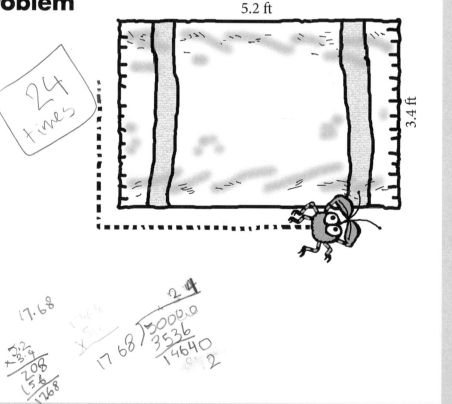

5.2 ft

3.4 ft

17.68
3.2
x 3.4
208
158
1268

24
17 68 ) 500 0.0
3536
14640
2

**1.** Rewrite this problem using the inverse operation.

**94 x 86 = 8084**

$8084 \div 94 = 86$

**2.** A chord that passes through the center of a circle is a

(a.) diameter    c. tangent

   b. radius      d. circumference

**3.** Write the expression to match the words:

**the difference between seventy and three times a number (x)**

$3x - 70$

**4.** List all the possible outcomes for the toss of one die (from a pair of dice).

(1,1)   (1,2)   (1,3)   (1,4)   (1,5)   (1,6)
(2,1)   (2,2)   (2,3)   (2,4)   (2,5)   (2,6)
(3,1)   (3,2)   (3,3)   (3,4)   (3,5)   (3,6)
(4,1)   (4,2)   (4,3)   (4,4)   (4,5)   (4,6)
(5,1)   (5,2)   (5,3)   (5,4)   (5,5)   (5,6)
(6,1)   (6,2)   (6,3)   (6,4)   (6,5)   (6,6)

**5.** **Dustin Phillips of Topeka, California, is the world's fastest ketchup drinker. He drank just over 90 percent of a 400-gram bottle of ketchup in 33 seconds.**

Ketch up with me.

Use mental math only to estimate . . .

   a. how much ketchup he drank

   b. how much ketchup he drank per second

**1.** Compute:
$$55.007 - 9.266$$
$45.741$

**2.** Circle the composite numbers.

2   (9)   17   51   (30)   23   (80)

**3.** Fill in the missing number.

$-2 + 19 + \boxed{-7} = 10$

**4.** Which angles are > 180°?

They EAT eggs?

**5.** How many teams ate fewer than half as many raw eggs as the Orange Team?

### Raw Egg Eating Contest — Results

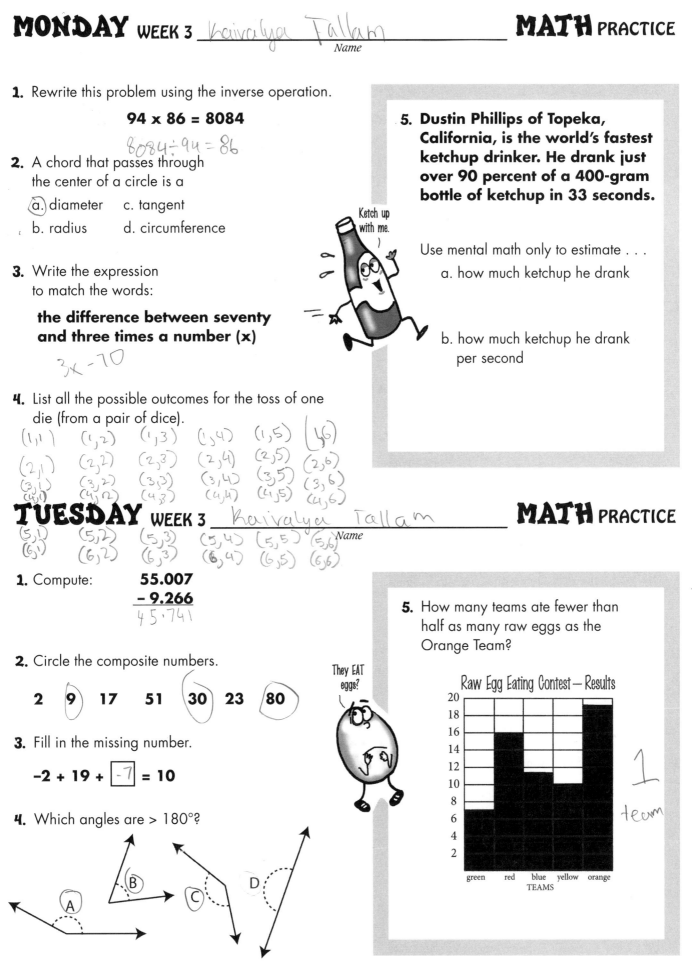

1 team

**1.** **273.55 – (–99.04) =**

    a. –174.51    c. 174.51

    (b.) 372.59    d. –372.59

**2.** Is this reasonable?

A man in India holds the world record for swallowing earthworms. In 2002, he swallowed 200 worms in 30 minutes. Someone calculates that, at this rate, he can swallow about 9,600 worms a day. *Yes*

**3.** Compute:     **–560 ÷ –70 =** 8

**4.** What kind of graph would be the best choice to represent data that shows an increase (each year) over a ten-year period in the number of worms the champion can swallow?

    a. line graph    c. double bar graph

    b. circle graph    d. pictograph

**5.** Which figures do NOT show symmetry?

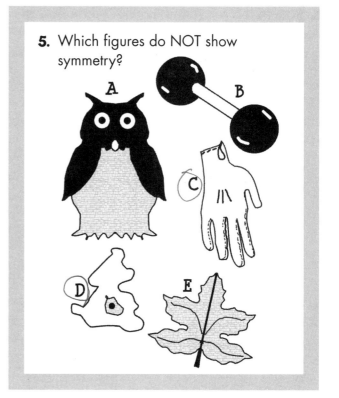

**1.** Use words to write this expression:

$$5(n-12)$$

*5 times n minus twelve*

**2.** Compute:     $\frac{3}{8} \div \frac{2}{3} = \frac{9}{16}$

**3.** Convert the measurement:

    **90 kg = _90,000_ g**

**4.** Which are the **common multiples** of 5 and 3?

    60    45    30    21

    18    40    36    (15)

**5.** Set up a proportion that could be used to solve this problem.

At the world's largest annual food fight, people throw tons of tomatoes at each other for fun. The record was set when 38,000 people threw 120 tons of tomatoes in an hour. At this rate, what was the weight of tomatoes thrown by 2,000 people?

*Name*

**1.** Estimate the solution:

182 – 97 + 1306 – 110 = 1281

95 + 1196

**2.** Find the average of these numbers.

**27, 19, 12, 80, 22, 170**

55

**3.** What are the **common factors** of **56** and **28**?

1, 2, 4, 7, 14, 28

**4.** Which equation matches the words?

**A number squared, multiplied by seven is one hundred eight more than the number.**

a.   $(7x)^2 = 108 + x$

b.   $7 + x^2 = x + 108$

c.   $7x^2 = y + 108$

d.   $7(x^2) = x + 108$

Do you like my hat?

# 5. Challenge Problem

He's going crackers!

A man named Ambrose Mendy, from the United Kingdom, is the world's fastest cream cracker eater. He set the record by consuming three crackers in 49.15 seconds. He broke the record of someone who took 79.25 seconds to eat three cream crackers.

If Ambrose claimed that his average time for eating one cracker was 20 seconds faster than the time of the previous record-holder, would his claim be accurate?

Explain your answer.

NO Because
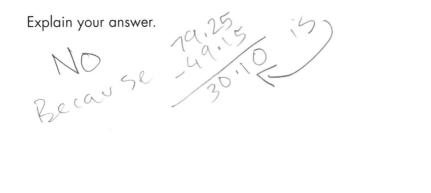
79.25
–49.15
30.10

Use It! Don't Lose It! IP 613-3

3/4

1. Compute:  **3800 x 2000 =** 7 600 000

2. The fastest speed recorded by a steam locomotive engine is 125 miles per hour. Another steam engine traveled $\frac{4}{5}$ as fast. What was the difference in the speeds?

3. Fill in the missing number.

**–10.01 x** -5 **= 50.05**

4. Which transformation is shown here?

a. slide      (b.) flip      c. turn

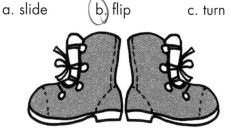

5. On how many days did Train B travel a greater distance than Train A?   2 days

DISTANCE TRAVELED BY
2 TRAINS IN ONE WEEK

```
1200
1100
1000
 900
 800
 700
 600
 500
 400
 300
 200
 100
      S  M  T  W  TH  F  S
```

————— TRAIN A
·············· TRAIN B

1. Compute:

$$9.9\overline{)75.24}$$

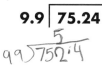

$$99\overline{)752.4}$$   5

I wish I could do math in my head.

2. Which metric measure is closest to six pounds?

(a.) 3 kg      b. 60 g      c. 10,000 g

3. What are the like terms in this equation?

**$5x^2 + 2y - x + 3x^2 = 302$**

$5x^2$  $3x^2$

4. Is this statement true or false?

**All these numbers are divisible by 6:
48, 72, 90, 188, and 258**

 False

5. Use trial and error to find the solution to this problem.

Two trains begin journeys 1,870 miles apart on parallel tracks.

Train A travels west at a speed of 90 mph. Train B travels east at a speed of 80 mph.

How much time will it take for the trains to meet?

# WEDNESDAY WEEK 4 _____    MATH PRACTICE
*Name*

**1.** Which number has the greater absolute value:

   **19 or –28?**  *-28*

**2.** Compute:   **37 + –12 – (–9) =**  *34*

**3.** Translate the problem into an equation
and find a solution.

   **The *Black Phantom* train has twice
   as many cars as the *Silver Streak*.
   Together, they have 87 cars. How many
   cars does the *Black Phantom* have?**

   *58 cars*   *x = 2y  x+y=87*
   *2y+y=87  3y=87  y=29*

**4.** Which figure is NOT a prism?

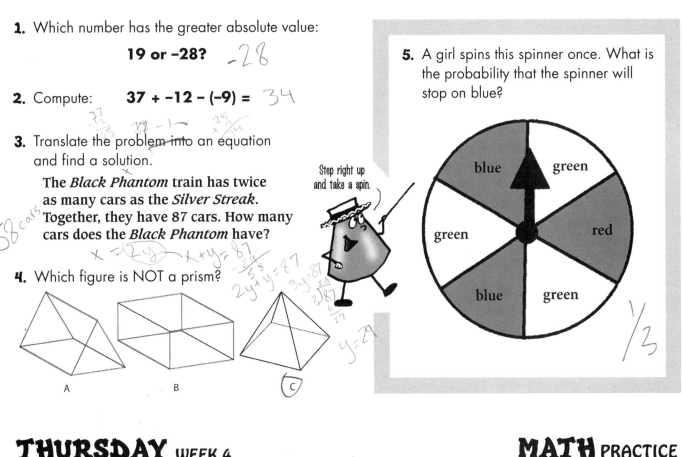

A          B          C

*Step right up
and take a spin.*

**5.** A girl spins this spinner once. What is
the probability that the spinner will
stop on blue?

blue    green

green          red

blue    green

*1/3*

# THURSDAY WEEK 4 _____    MATH PRACTICE
*Name*

**1.** A travel company brags that 94 percent
of its trains are on time. The company
runs 250 train trips a week. How many
are on time?

   *224*

*Timing is
everything.*

*94)25000  255
188
620
574
460*

**2.** Write an expression to match the words:

   **a number (x) squared divided by
   four times another number**

   *x²/4y*

**3.** The value of **9³** is _____ *729*

   *81
   x 9
   729*

**4.** Finish the number sentence to demonstrate
the commutative property of addition.

   $\frac{7}{9} + \frac{3}{5} =$  *35/45 + 27/45 = 62/45*

   *1 17/45*

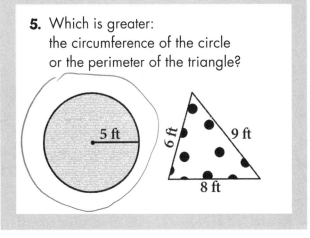

**5.** Which is greater:
the circumference of the circle
or the perimeter of the triangle?

5 ft    6 ft    9 ft    8 ft

**1.** Is this answer correct?

$$\frac{9}{5} \div \frac{2}{3} = 2\frac{7}{10}$$

**2.** Which operation should be done first when solving the following problem?

**8(5 + 2) – 13 =**

I get right to the point.

**3.** Simplify the expression.

**8d + 17 – 2d – 12**

**4.** Find the area of this figure.

15 m

22 m

## 5. Challenge Problem

Charlie and Max love to ride trains. The table shows the number of trips they have taken in the first nine months of the year. Look for the pattern in the data. Explain the pattern. Then tell what the numbers will be for each of them in September through December if their trips follow the same pattern.

Just keep chugging along.

| Month | Charlie | Max |
|-------|---------|-----|
| J | 2 | 0 |
| F | 5 | 1 |
| M | 8 | 3 |
| A | 11 | 6 |
| My | 14 | 10 |
| Jn | 17 | 15 |
| Jy | 20 | 21 |
| A | 23 | 28 |
| S | | |
| O | | |
| N | | |
| D | | |

*Name*

3/11

**1.** Compute:

48 ) 12,480   *260*
360
96
288
288

**2.** A roller coaster has nine cars. Each car holds four people. A school group has 135 sixth graders. How many trips will the coaster have to take to give a ride to all the students?

36 ) 136   *3 trips*
108
98

**3.** Simplify the expression:

**8(a + b) – 3b + 12**

8a + 8b - 3b + 12
*8a + 5b + 2*

**4.** A triangle has two or more congruent sides. What kind of triangle could it be?

Isoceles Triangle

**5.** Which ride carries the most passengers in a 30-minute period?

### Riders at the Village of Thrills

| Ride | # of passengers | Duration of Ride |
|------|------|------|
| *Circle Mania* | 22 | 6 min |
| *Speeding Bullet* | 16 | 5 min |
| *Runaway Train* | 20 | 4 min |
| *Splish-Splash* | 36 | 9 min |

*Name*

3/12

**1.** Max plays a game at the amusement park. He is told that four of the nine boxes contain a prize. He chooses a box. What are the odds against getting a prize?

$\frac{5}{9}$

**2.** Compute: **$194.16 x 3 =**

$582.48

**3.** Write this number in words: **6,060,606**

six million, sixty thousand six hundred and six

**4.** Sue throws darts at this target. What is its area?

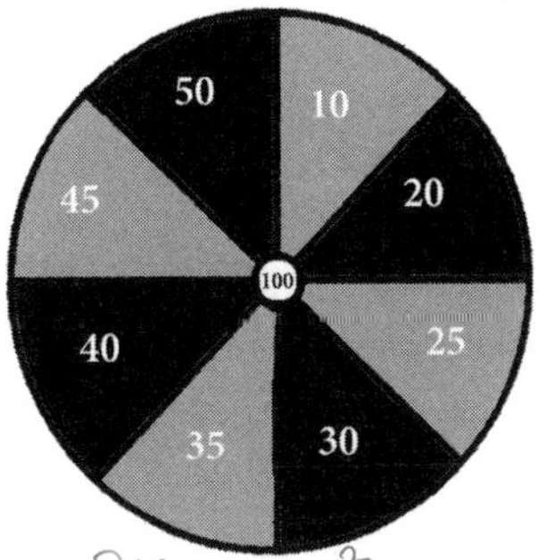

3.14
64
1256
1884
200.96 cm²

The target is 16" in diameter.

**5.** Charlie took three times as many rides on the *Rock & Roller Coaster* as Tom. Sue rode seven times. This was $\frac{1}{4}$ of the combined rides of Charlie and Tom.

Which equation matches the statement?

○ **3x – 7 = 4**

● **$\frac{1}{4}$(x + 3x) = 7**

○ **4(x + 7) = 3x**

○ **$\frac{x + 3}{4}$ = 7**

3/13

**1.** On a wild water ride, Amy lost ten coins totaling 76¢. What could those coins have been? Find two different answers.

2 quarters, 6 pennies, 2 dimes

**2.** Write an expression to match the words:

**negative five times the sum of a number (n) and fourteen**

$-5(14+n)$

**3.** Compute:   $-48 + 76 + 3 - (-9) =$   40

$\begin{array}{r} {}^{6}_{7}6 \\ -48 \\ \hline 28 \end{array} + 3 + 9 = 31 + 9 = 40$

**4.** Someone tosses a penny while another person tosses one die. List all the possible outcomes of the two events.

H,1   T,1
H,2   T,2
H,3   T,3
H,4   T,4
H,5   T,5
H,6   T,6

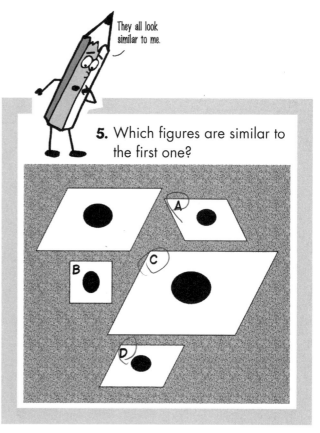

They all look similar to me.

**5.** Which figures are similar to the first one?

3/14

**1.** Which measurement statements are reasonable?

    a. A basketball weighs 30 kg.

    b. A doorknob is 30 cm wide.

    c. A birdbath holds 10 L of water.

    d. A snail crawls 1 m in an hour.

**2.** Compute:   $\frac{9}{5} \times \frac{7}{11} = \frac{63}{55} = 1\frac{8}{55}$

**3.** Which number is forty-four and four hundred four thousandths?

    a. 44.044     b. 44.404     c. 44.0404

**4.** Finish the number pattern.

90, 30, 60, 0, 30, –30, 0, __-60__, __-30__

**5.** After buying tickets for rides, Sandy has 12 quarters, 7 dimes, 15 nickels, and 9 pennies. Cotton candy costs $1.25 each. Does she have enough money to buy a cotton candy for herself and two friends?

3.75     $\begin{array}{r} 70 \\ 1.25 \end{array}$     Yes

1.95

I'm worth more than you!

*Name*

3/15

**1.** How many faces are there on a pyramid with a rectangular base?

5 faces

**2.** Compute:  **136 x 258 =**

    a. 25,088

    b. 34,988

    c. 35,088

    d. 35,078

I never calculated on that.

**3.** Fill in the missing operation.

**0.14 ☒ 57.05 = 7.987**

**4.** Write an equation that can be used to solve this problem.

**Four friends took a total of 95 rides on attractions at the amusement park. Al took 12 rides. Val and Sal rode the same number of times. Mel rode four times fewer than Val. How many times did Sal ride?**

$V = 5$

$M = V - 4$

$A = 12$

$V + M + A + S = 95$

## 5. Challenge Problem

Draw a bar graph to show this data.
Be sure to include a title and labels.

Cotton Candy Sales

Cotton Candy Sales
1st week in July

| | |
|---|---|
| S | 1230 |
| M | 575 |
| T | 420 |
| W | 762 |
| Th | 785 |
| F | 990 |
| Sa | 1530 |

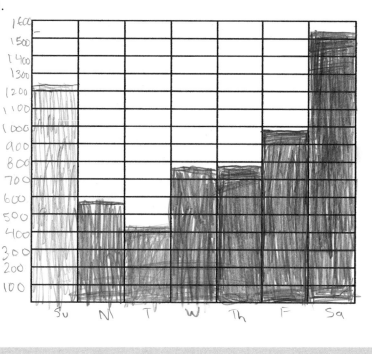

*Name*

3/18

**1.** Simplify the expression:

$$60 + 9p - 46 - p$$

14 + 8p

**2.** By the time the campers went to sleep, the temperature was 2° F. By morning, the temperature was –9° F. Write and solve a subtraction problem to find the difference between the two temperatures.

-9 - 2 = -11      11° F

**3.** Compute:

26

26

$$974 \overline{)25,324}$$

1948

5844

5844

**4.** Define a **ray**. Draw one.

Did you say to draw one?

**5.** Finish the tree diagram to show the possible outcomes of the two events: drawing a bill from a box that has one of each ($100, $50, $20) and drawing a marble from a bag that has equal numbers of red, yellow, and green.

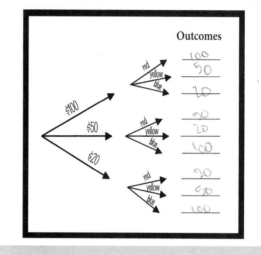

Outcomes
100
50
20
90
20
100
90
50
100

*Name*

3/19

**1.** Fill in the missing symbol: <, >, or =

$$9,0909 \boxed{>} 9.0099$$

**2.** Show three other ways to represent the value of this number. Use words, numerals, and/or symbols.

**0.75**

25%    zero point seventy five    75%

3/4    75¢

**3.** Compute: **26.015 x 3.4 =** 88.451

**4.** Find the area of this figure.

1020 cm    27

20 cm

38 cm

**5.** What information in the problem is NOT needed in order to find a solution?

Twelve hikers set out on a 12-mile hike to a lake. The hike involved an elevation change of 2,300 feet. ~~The average age of the hikers was 15.~~ The first hiker got to the lake in 3.75 hours. What was this hiker's rate (per hour) of walking?

All this hiking is hard on the sole.

361 + 400 = c²

761 = c²    √761 =

3/20

**1.** Write this equation:

the square root of a number (n)
divided by four equals thirty-nine

$\frac{\sqrt{n}}{4} = 39$

**2.** Compute:  **63 x –9 =** −567

$\frac{54}{\frac{3}{76}}$

**3.** The number of times a given item occurs in a set
of data is
- ◉ the frequency    ○ the sampling
- ○ the median      ○ the range

**4.** Is **76** a reasonable solution to this problem?

Eleven hikers all had the same number
of mosquito bites. The total number of
bites was 407. How many bites did
each hiker have?

$\begin{array}{r} 76 \\ \times 11 \\ \hline 76 \\ 760 \\ \hline 836 \end{array}$  NO

**5.** Which figure is congruent to
the first one?

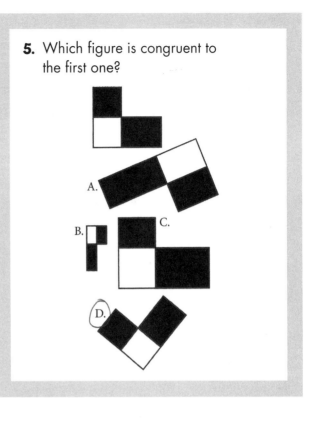

A.

B.    C.

D.

3/21

**1.** Which statements are true?
- ✓ a. All numbers are natural numbers.
- ___ b. A decimal is a rational number.
- ___ c. A fraction cannot be an integer.
- ✓ d. An exponential number is a real number.

**2.** What is the coefficient in the equation?

$$\frac{20}{11k} + 5 = \frac{1}{3}$$

Let me think....?

$\frac{20}{11}$

**3.** Compute:  $15\frac{3}{8} - 6\frac{7}{8} =$

$14\frac{11}{8} - 6\frac{7}{8} = 8\frac{4}{8} = 8\frac{1}{2}$

**4.** Which temperature shows the boiling point
of water?

( 100° F )    100° C    0° C    212° C

**5.** The hikers' packs got lighter as the trip
went along, because they ate their
food! Whose pack dropped more
weight during the trip than Allie's?

| Hiker | Pack Weight Beginning of Trip (lbs) | Pack Weight End of Trip (lbs) |
|---|---|---|
| Tad | 42 | 36 |
| Chris | 38 | 32 |
| Alex | 47 | 40 |
| Allie | 43 | 38 |
| Tom | 39 | 37 |
| Tara | 37 | 33 |

**1.** Estimate the answer

3/22

$21.6 + 38.2 + 794 - 52 =$ 742 + 59.8

801.8

**3.** Compute:

$36 - \frac{9 + 12}{7} =$ 36 - 3 = 33

**2.** Define the term: ***dependent events.***

**4.** Find **x** if **y** = 30.

$2y + 102 = 2x^2$

60 + 102 = 2x²

$\frac{162}{2} = 2x^2$

81 = x² = x = √81 = 9

---

## 5. Challenge Problem

Draw a diagram to find the solution.

**Five hikers are walking down a trail toward a campsite. Who is in the lead?**

You can use stick figures in your diagram.

Clues:

- Dana and Jane are behind Rachael.
- Kris is ahead of Georgia.
- There are two hikers between Rachael and Jane.
- Georgia is ahead of Jane, but slower than Pam.
- Pam is behind Kris.
- Jane is ahead of Dana.

K  G

R    J    D

Kris

3/25

**1.** Which is NOT true of all rectangles?

    a. They have four equal sides.

    b. They have four right angles.

    c. The opposite angles are congruent.

**2.** Simplify the equation.

$$\frac{70d}{5} + d - 12 = 33$$

**3.** Use the inverse operation to check the accuracy of this answer. Show your work.

$$186 \times 42 = 7{,}812$$

7812 ÷ 42 = 186

**4.** A diver rises to the surface in 3.76 minutes. A second diver takes 5.922 minutes longer. How long does the second diver take to surface?

9.682 min

**5.** Give the coordinates of all the fish.

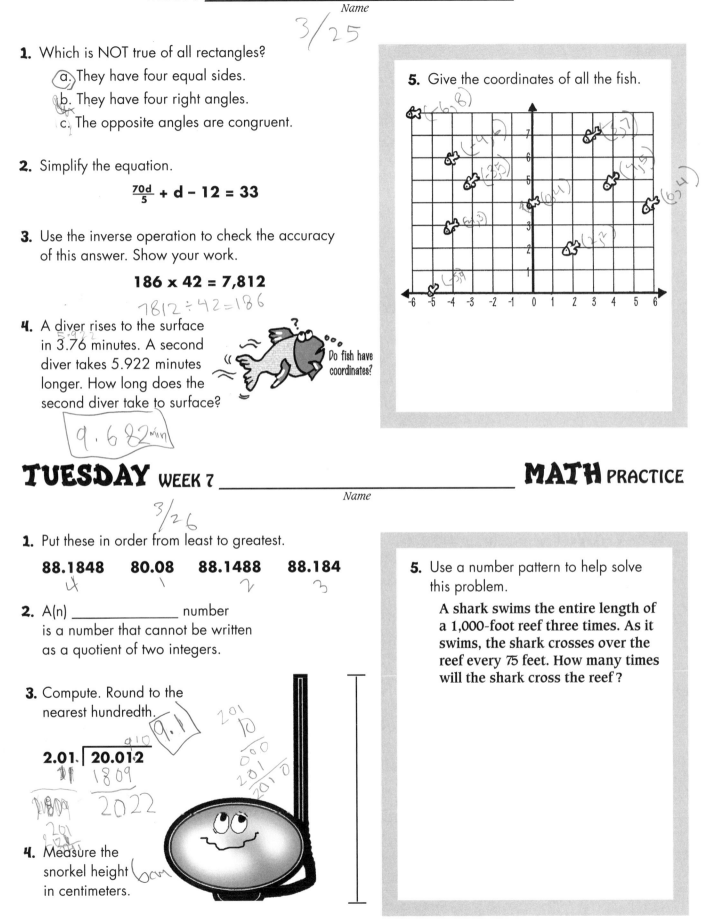

Do fish have coordinates?

3/26

**1.** Put these in order from least to greatest.

    88.1848    80.08    88.1488    88.184

    4        1        2        3

**2.** A(n) _____ number is a number that cannot be written as a quotient of two integers.

**3.** Compute. Round to the nearest hundredth.

$$2.01\overline{)20.012}$$

**4.** Measure the snorkel height in centimeters.

**5.** Use a number pattern to help solve this problem.

    A shark swims the entire length of a 1,000-foot reef three times. As it swims, the shark crosses over the reef every 75 feet. How many times will the shark cross the reef?

**1.** Compute:     $-70\overline{\smash{\big)}63{,}350}$

**2.** An obtuse angle
measures between _____° and _____° .

**3.** Solve the equation:

   $x - (-7) = 95$

**4.** The deck of a boat is three feet
above the surface. A diver leaves the
deck and descends to a depth of
–47.5 feet. Write a problem to find
the difference between the deck and
the diver's deepest underwater point.

I can calculate
this problem
in 13.25 seconds.

**5.** A diver selects a mask and a life vest
from different bags without looking
into the bags. He chooses one mask
from a bag that contains two blue and
two green masks. He chooses a life
vest from a bag that has one orange
and three yellow vests. What is the
probability that he will get a yellow
vest and a blue mask?

**1.** Put these in order from least to greatest.

   $\dfrac{3}{4}$        $\dfrac{2}{3}$        $\dfrac{5}{8}$        $\dfrac{5}{7}$

**2.** Anna saw 171 fish during her 38-minute dive.
At this rate, how many did she see in the first
two minutes?

**3.** Compute:     $\dfrac{5}{12} \div \dfrac{2}{5} =$

**4.** Find the area
of this figure:

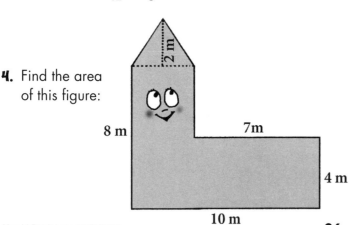

**5.** Can this equation be used to solve
the following problem?
*(Use t to stand for time.)*

   $t = 50 + t^2$

**Alex stayed underwater three
minutes on his first scuba dive.
The next day, his underwater time
was 50 minutes more than the
square of the first day's time.
How long did he stay underwater?**

**1.** Is the answer correct?
If not, correct it.

926
37
404
818
92
100
202
+ 699

3,288

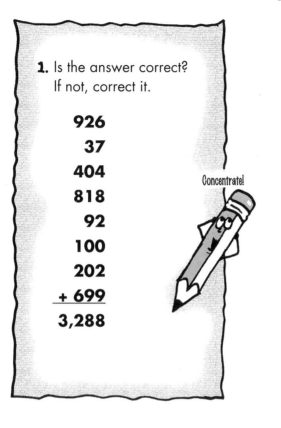

Concentrate!

**2.** Tell what is meant by the **odds in favor** of an outcome. Then decide if the following statement below about odds in favor is true.

Alex is missing a size 8 swim fin. Eighteen swim fins are thrown in a basket on the boat. Eleven are size 8. Four are size 7, and three are size 9. Someone grabs a fin randomly and brings it to Alex.

*The odds in favor of Alex getting the right size fin are $\frac{3}{15}$.*

**3.** What number has the opposite value from **742.55**?

**4.** Compute:  **$3,000.00 – $1,683.25**

# 5. Challenge Problem

Use a trial and error strategy to solve this problem.

Two years ago, Sam was two-thirds of Pam's age (at that time). In three years, Sam will be three-fourths of Pam's age. In 20 years, the sum of their ages will be 69. How old is Sam?

How old is Pam?

I know! I know!

How old is Sam?

**1.** At the airport, Molly finds a gumball machine with three green, six red, and six blue gumballs. She puts in her quarter and gets a red gumball. She puts in another quarter for a second gumball. What is the probability that the second gumball will be blue?

**2.** Simplify:  **$2b + 4b^2 + 2b = 16$**

**3.** Moe drove 1,545 miles in three days. She drove 412 miles on Monday and 495 miles on Wednesday. How far did she drive on Tuesday?

**4.** Angle A and Angle B are **complementary angles**. Angle B measures 53°. What is the measure of Angle A?

**5.** The table shows the distances (in miles) that Yoko, a yoyo salesman, traveled in six months. What was his average distance per month?

| month | miles |
|-------|-------|
| Jan | 480 |
| Feb | 1659 |
| Mar | 5747 |
| Apr | 713 |
| May | 2004 |
| Jun | 995 |

**1.** Compute: $\sqrt{144} - \sqrt{121} =$

**2.** What is the surface area of a 20 cm cube?

    8,000 cm$^3$       2,400 cm$^2$

    2,400 cm$^3$       8,000 cm$^2$

**3.** Solve the equation: **$107x = 802.5$**

**4.** Round to the nearest whole number:

    **$699\frac{5}{6}$**

**5.** Fred drove from his home in Boston, MA to Miami, FL. His trip took 99 hours and 50 minutes (including stopping time). He arrived in Miami at 2:10 pm on Friday. What time (and day) did he leave home?

I'm running out of time.

Tick Tick Tick

**1.** Estimate the total time of Tess's trip.

**Tess drove 55 minutes to the airport. She waited an hour and 45 minutes for her plane. The flight took three hours and 14 minutes. It took an hour and five minutes to walk to baggage claim, get her suitcase, and pick up a rental car. She drove 48 minutes to her friend's house.**

**2.** Compute:  **35 + –84 =**

**3.** Fill in the missing sign: <, >, or =

**–12 – (–60) + 8** ▢ **2(–40 + 18)**

**4.** Name two real-life objects that are **cylinders**.

**5.** All these non-stop flights leave Philadelphia for cities in the same time zone. Which flight is the longest?

| Destination | Flight # | Depart | Arrive |
|---|---|---|---|
| Atlanta | 2117 | 7:52 p | 9:35 p |
| Newark | 96 | 8:30 a | 10:13 a |
| Tampa | 265 | 11:45 a | 2:54 p |
| Albany | 171 | 3:35 p | 4:47 p |
| Roanoke | 12 | 12:10 p | 1:36 p |

Sorry, I'm a little slow today.

**1.** Compute:  $\frac{3}{8} \times \frac{12}{15} =$

**2.** C.J. claims that he covered a distance of 3200 kilometers on a one-day bike trip. Is this a reasonable measurement?

**3.** Circle fractions equivalent to $\frac{5}{6}$.

$\frac{15}{21}$   $\frac{2}{3}$   $\frac{60}{70}$   $\frac{100}{120}$   $\frac{75}{90}$

No problem!

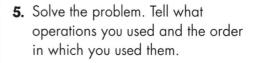

**4.** Is this solution correct?

**–168y = 168,000**

**y = 1000**

**5.** Solve the problem. Tell what operations you used and the order in which you used them.

**An airplane had a total of 168 seats. There were six seats in each row. Half of the rows were full of passengers. The rest of the rows had two empty seats in each row. How many passengers were seated on the plane?**

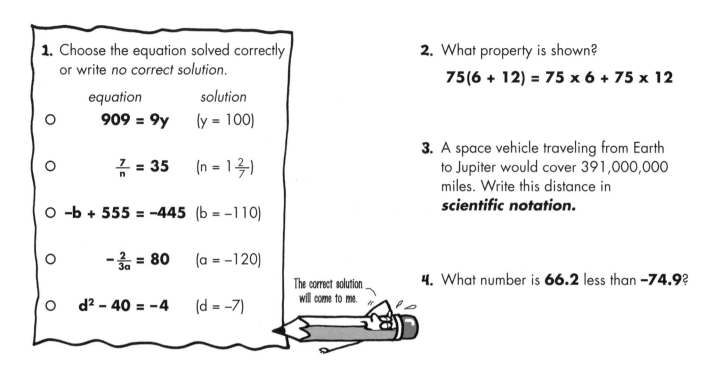

1. Choose the equation solved correctly or write *no correct solution.*

   | | equation | solution |
   |---|---|---|
   | ○ | **909 = 9y** | (y = 100) |
   | ○ | $\frac{7}{n} = 35$ | (n = $1\frac{2}{7}$) |
   | ○ | **–b + 555 = –445** | (b = –110) |
   | ○ | $-\frac{2}{3a} = 80$ | (a = –120) |
   | ○ | **d² – 40 = –4** | (d = –7) |

The correct solution will come to me.

2. What property is shown?

   **75(6 + 12) = 75 x 6 + 75 x 12**

3. A space vehicle traveling from Earth to Jupiter would cover 391,000,000 miles. Write this distance in **scientific notation.**

4. What number is **66.2** less than **–74.9**?

## 5. Challenge Problem

On her beach vacation, Sue has picked up lots of shells and stored them in small boxes that are five-inch cubes. Each of the 65 boxes is completely filled with shells. Now she is packing the shells into a suitcase. She wants to keep the shells in the boxes. Sue is sure she can fit all these boxes of shells in her suitcase. Is she right?

If not, how many boxes of shells can she fit into this suitcase? *(Note: The dimensions given are for the inside of the suitcase.)*

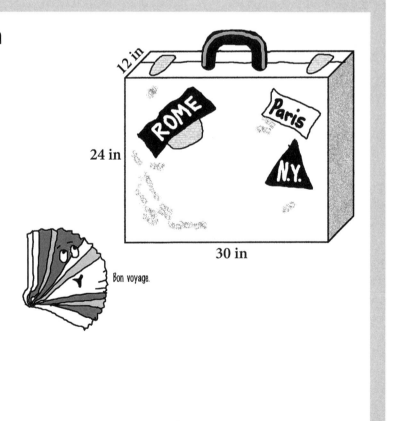

12 in

24 in

30 in

Bon voyage.

**1.** Solve the equation. **400 = –80p**

You'll skate right through these problems.

**2.** There are two blue hats, three green hats, one black hat, and two white hats in the closet. Matt grabs a ski hat from the closet without looking. What is the probability that the hat he grabs will **not** be green?

**3.** Which operation should be done first?

$-6 + 9(10 + 3^2) - 7 =$

**4.** How many edges are on a rectangular prism?

**5.** Five figure skaters go to the ice rink to practice. Rob stays two hours and ten minutes. Brie takes a hard fall and leaves after 210 seconds. Brett stays three quarters of an hour. Maria practices for 270 minutes. Jude stays an hour and a half. What is the total practice time of all five skaters?

Explain the strategy you would use to solve this problem.

**1.** Which fractions are in lowest terms?

$\frac{7}{9}$          $\frac{3}{6}$          $\frac{8}{10}$

$\frac{19}{21}$          $\frac{6}{9}$          $\frac{8}{5}$

**2.** How many **variables** are in this expression?

$5a + 12b + 3a^2 - a$

**3.** Compute: **0.073 + 10.1909 =**

**4.** Find the volume of this figure.

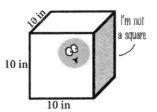

10 in
10 in
10 in
I'm not a square.

**5.** Is this a problem that can be solved?

**The fastest speed by a female skier is 234.528 kilometers per hour. The fastest speed by a male skier is 248.105 kilometers per hour. What is the difference between these speeds?**

*Name*

1. Which is the correct way to simplify the equation?

    **$20k - k - 3 - 3k^2 = 22 + 3$**

    a. $19k - 3k^2 - 3 = 25$

    b. $22k - 3 = 25$

    c. $19k - 3k^2 = 28$

    d. $16k - 3 = 25$

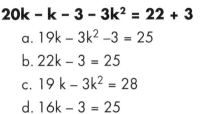

The best way to simplify is to lose a few digits!

4. Find the **mode** of this set of data.

| Ski Race Times (in seconds) | | | | |
|---|---|---|---|---|
| 7 | 12 | 15 | 19 | 9 |
| 3 | 8 | 12 | 17 | 21 |
| 12 | 6 | 15 | 11 | 25 |
| 10 | 18 | 13 | 12 | 22 |

2. Sixteen snowboarders each spent $250 on a season ticket to Snowbird Mountain. They figured out that they spent $4,000. Are they right?

5. Draw two different parallelograms with no right angles.

3. Compute:     **$-350 \times -7 =$**

*Name*

1. List the common factors of **12** and **48**.

    Circle the **greatest common factor.**

2. Fill in the missing operation.

    $$\frac{11}{7} \, \boxed{\phantom{x}} \, \frac{6}{9} = 2\frac{5}{14}$$

3. What unit or units would be good choices for measuring the amount of hot chocolate in a mug?

Develop a taste for math.

4. Simplify the equation:

    **$y = n^4 \times n^6$**

5. Which year had 2 m less snow than 2004?

### Snowfall at Mt. Blanco Snowboard Area

| 2000 | ✳ ✳ ✳ ⸯ |
|---|---|
| 2001 | ✳ ✳ ⸯ |
| 2002 | ✳ ✳ ⸸ |
| 2003 | ✳ ✳ ⸰ |
| 2004 | ✳ ✳ ✳ ⸸ |

2 meters = ✳

**1.** Estimate the solution:

**88 x 515 =**

**2.** Which conversions are correct?

    a.        5 qt = 20 C

    b.      6.6 m = 660 cm

    c.     2 mi = 10,560 ft

    d.    48 oz = 4 lb

    e.     30 L = 30,000 mL

    f.     606 g = 60.6 kg

    g.  1,000 lb = 10,000 oz

    h.   7.5 gal = 15 qt

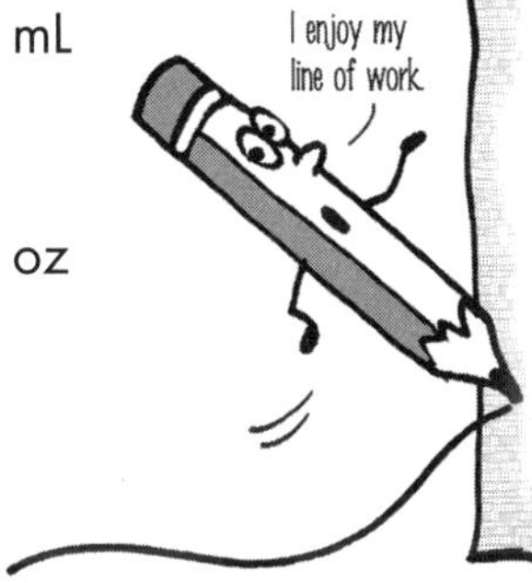

*I enjoy my line of work.*

**3.** Compute: **60,000 ÷ 50 =**

**4.** Solve the equation. Show all your steps. Describe each step in words.

**38n − 66 = 86**

## 5. Challenge Problem

Draw the next four figures to continue the pattern.

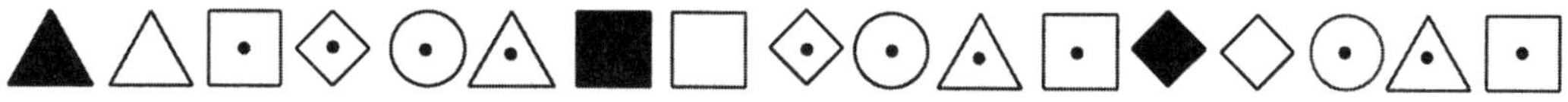

▲ △ ⊡ ◇ ⊙ △ ■ □ ◇ ⊙ △ ⊡ ◆ ◇ ⊙ △ ⊡

_____ _____ _____ _____

# MONDAY WEEK 10 ______________________________ MATH PRACTICE
Name

1. Compute: 65,036 + 9,893

Math is fun.

2. Solve the equation.

$$\frac{3}{5}y - \frac{2}{5}y = 50$$

3. What is the ***median*** in a set of data?

4. Draw a ***slide*** of this figure.

5. Solve the problem. Tell what operations were needed and the order in which you used them.

**The highest sand dune ever measured was 1,526 feet high. Another dune was 163 high. During a storm, 73 feet of sand were added to it. How much more sand would it need to accumulate in order to be as tall as the highest sand dune?**

# TUESDAY WEEK 10 ______________________________ MATH PRACTICE
Name

1. Shana pitched her tent in the desert. In the first day, she saw 18 spiders and 12 rats. What is the ratio of rats to spiders?

2. Compute and round to nearest hundredth.

**10.33 x 115.09 =**

3. What formula would be used to find the volume of a cylindrical water container?

4. A camel caravan treks the width of the Sahara Desert: 3,200 miles. This is about:

   a. 5100 kilometers c. 500 kilometers
   b. 1920 kilometers d. 2000 kilometers

5. Fill in the blanks to finish the pattern.

| Day | Daytime Temp, F | Nighttime Temp, F |
|---|---|---|
| S | 68 | 45 |
| M | 71 | 48 |
| T | 75 | 52 |
| W | | 57 |
| Th | 86 | |
| F | | 70 |
| S | 101 | |

Oops, I think I'd better start again.

 

**1.** Sasha has four different-colored jackets in her closet: blue, red, green, and yellow. She packs two jackets for her safari. How many different combinations are possible?

**2.** Compute:    $7\overline{)-48,174}$

**3.** True or false?

**A chord is a line segment joining two points on a circle and passing through the center.**

**4.** Simplify the equation.

$$9 + w^2 + 6 + 4w^2 = 35$$

**5.** Four people want to share this stew. Rewrite the recipe to serve four.

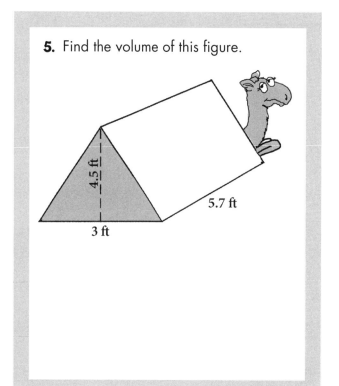

## Desert Stew
### serves 12

$4\frac{1}{2}$ C cactus chunks
8 C crushed tumbleweed
$9\frac{3}{4}$ C cactus juice
12 lizard eggs, raw
$6\frac{3}{4}$ T crumbled flower petals
10 qt. water

Combine all ingredients and boil over low heat for an hour.

*This recipe strikes just the right chord.*

**1.** Which operation should be done first?

$$7(b + 9) - 16 + (-5) =$$

**2.** Tom's bank account balance is –$95.13. Terry's balance is –$37.25. Write and solve a problem to find the difference.

**3.** Compute:    $\frac{3}{5} \div \frac{9}{10}$

**4.** A camel that weighs 1,250 pounds has a hump containing 80 pounds of fat. What percentage of the camel's total weight is contained in that fat?

**5.** Find the volume of this figure.

4.5 ft

3 ft

5.7 ft

**1.** Compute:  $\frac{4}{5} \times 700.49 =$

Round your answer to the nearest tenth.

**2.** If x = 8, what is y?

$$x + \frac{4x}{2} = -y$$

**3.** Compute:  **$7,512.78 ÷ 3 =**

**4.** Which figure is **congruent** to the first one?

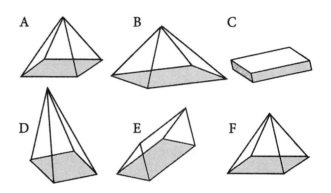

A    B    C

D    E    F

## 5. Challenge problem

Solve the problem by working backwards.

*This problem is a snap.*

Guide Alana took a group of ten tourists out on a safari trip to take pictures of animals. The group left base camp early in the morning.

They traveled 45 minutes before stopping to take pictures of some giraffes. The stop lasted 39 minutes. Then they traveled an hour and 10 minutes to a riverbank where they took a rest stop for 32 minutes. Back in the jeeps, they drove 37 minutes until they came upon a herd of elephants. They stopped and watched the elephants for an hour and 15 minutes.

The trip resumed with 15 minutes of travel before lunch. They stopped in a shady spot for an hour-long lunch break. After lunch, the group drove for 72 more minutes and stopped to watch animals for 125 minutes before arriving back at the base camp at 5:25 p.m.

What time did they leave camp in the morning? _____

What time did they stop for lunch? _____

**1.** Nick, a skateboarder, won 27 of the 36 competitions he entered. What percent of the competitions did he win?

**2.** Compute:     **3737 ÷ 37 =**

**3.** Dan, Stan, and Nan raced on their skateboards. How many permutations are there for the order in which the race could have been finished?

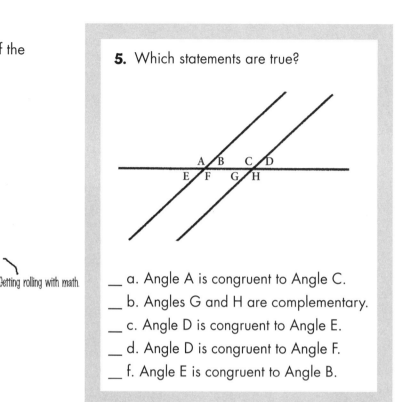

_Getting rolling with math._

**4.** Use words to write this expression.

$30 + 9(p^3 - 7)$

**5.** Which statements are true?

___ a. Angle A is congruent to Angle C.
___ b. Angles G and H are complementary.
___ c. Angle D is congruent to Angle E.
___ d. Angle D is congruent to Angle F.
___ f. Angle E is congruent to Angle B.

**1.** Kate took all the change she had saved and went shopping for a used skateboard. She had 185 quarters, 370 dimes, 216 nickels, and 135 pennies. Could she buy a board that cost $94.95?

**2.** Compute:

**0.66 ÷ 2.541**

**3.** Simplify the equation.

$$\frac{b^2}{8} + 13 = 31$$

**4.** Find the volume of this figure.

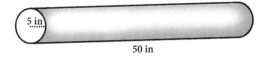

5 in

50 in

**5.** Use mental math to solve these problems.

A total of 210 people attended a town meeting to discuss the building of a skateboard park. Kids made up two-thirds of the audience; the rest were adults. Everyone was in favor of the park except for 20 percent of the adults.

a. How many were in favor of the park?

b. How many kids were present?

**1.** Compute: **–97 + 32 – (–11) =**

   a. 140      c. 54

   b. –54      d. –76

**2.** Solve the equation.

$$\frac{x}{30} = \frac{1}{2}$$

I'll probably land on my feet!

**3.** If you toss a pair of dice, what is the probability that you will not get two of the same number?

**4.** How many faces are found on a cone?

**5.**

### Skateboard Injuries
### Team Ashland, 2004–2005

| Type of Injury | 2004 | 2005 |
|---|---|---|
| scrapes & cuts | 165 | 130 |
| sprains | 29 | 40 |
| head injuries | 6 | 3 |
| broken bones | 9 | 10 |
| bruises | 200 | 130 |

Which injury occurred at least 50 percent less from 2004 to 2005?

**1.** Solve the proportion.

$$\frac{28}{4} = \frac{x}{60}$$

**2.** Compute:     $\frac{3}{7} + 1\frac{2}{9} =$

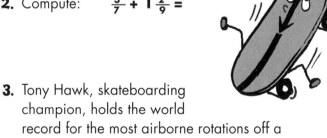

Roll on!

**3.** Tony Hawk, skateboarding champion, holds the world record for the most airborne rotations off a skateboard. His record performance was two and one-half full rotations. How many degrees is this?

**4.** Fill in the missing symbol: <, >, or =

$$\frac{9}{2} + \sqrt{121} \;\boxed{\phantom{x}}\; 5^2 - 9.5$$

**5.** George has practiced skateboard tricks for a number of days in a row. The number of days is a number with the characteristics listed below. Find three different possibilities for the number.

   • It is a 4-digit number.

   • It is an even number.

   • It is > 1,000 and < 1,500.

   • The sum of its digits is 8.

   • None of its digits is > 5.

**1.** Which examples do not show the ***identity property***?

    a. $942 \times 0 = 0$

    b. $36.8 \times 1 = 36.8$

    c. $\frac{3}{5} + 0 = \frac{3}{5}$

    d. $36 \times 1 = 6$

**2.** Is this solution accurate?

**$92,763 \div 7 = 13,251$ (R 5)**

**3.** Find z if w = −5.

**$8(w + 9) + 40 = z - 20$**

**4.** The graph shows how Simone spent a total of $480 on skateboard supplies. Estimate the amount she spent on the board.

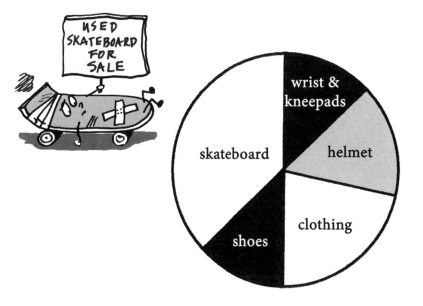

## 5. Challenge Problem

Solve the following problem.

Explain, in writing, the strategy you used to solve the problem.

**A committee begins planning an indoor skateboard competition. Several large areas are needed in which to set up ramps and courses. The committee considers renting an available arena that is 480 by 120 feet of open space. For the competition, they will need to provide 18 different areas. Ten of them must be 47 by 42 feet. The others need to be spaces that are 87 by 61 feet. Will this arena meet their needs?**

**Explain:**

Explanation

**1.** Alexa grabs a parachute from a box of 15 parachutes. There are seven yellow, three red, and five blue parachutes. What is the probability that she will choose one that is **not** yellow?

**2.** Simplify the equation.

$$7 + \frac{12x}{4} - 80 = 56$$

**3.** A type of graph that uses a grid to show relationships between two quantities is a

    O histogram      O tally sheet

    O scattergram      O pictograph

**4.** True or false?

**A trapezoid is a quadrilateral that has only one pair of parallel sides.**

**5.** Parachutist Don Kellner (USA) holds the world record for the most parachute jumps. From mid-1961 to mid-2003, he jumped 34,000 times. On average, how many times did he jump each year? *(Round the answer to the nearest whole number.)*

Jump right in!

**1.** The highest bungee jump from a hot air balloon is 15,200 feet. Approximately how many meters is this?

**2.** Compute:     **8.0634 x 10,000 =**

**3.** Use words to write this expression.

$$\frac{2x^3}{5} < 60$$

**4.** Round to the nearest tenth:

    **47.9634**

**5.** Which has the greater volume, the cone or the sphere?

8 cm

10 cm

8 cm

**1.** Compute:

$$-35\overline{\smash{)}-23{,}170}$$

Flying high!

**2.** What formula will solve the problem?

**The greatest distance (d) a hang glider has traveled at one time is about 435.2m. If this took eight hours (t), what was the rate (r) of travel per hour?**

**3.** Name this figure:

**4.** If you roll a pair of dice, what are the **odds against** getting snake eyes (two ones)?

**5.** Three sky-diving friends are competing to see who can stay in the air the longest. Each friend is wearing a different colored suit. Follow the clues to figure out how they placed.

- The second place person finished between the divers with the blue and green suits.
- Gabe wore a blue suit.
- Angela did not wear a red suit.
- Ralph did not finish third.
- Angela did not finish third.

**1.** Compute: $1\frac{5}{6} \times 5\frac{1}{5} =$

**2.** What is the **least common multiple** of six and eight?

I can calculate that!

**3.** Simplify the expression.

**8n + 7 − n − 98**

**4.** Solve the problem by translating it into an equation.

**Molly spent twice as many hours as Peyton in a hot air balloon. She spent 46 hours fewer than Kurt. The total for all three balloonists was 246 hours. How long did Kurt spend in the balloon?**

**5.** Estrid Geersten of Denmark is the oldest female to do a tandem parachute jump. She was born on August 1, 1904.

  a. How old was she when she did the record-setting jump on October 1, 2003?

  b. How old would she be today?

*Name*

**1.** Fill in the missing operation.

$$0.062 \boxed{\phantom{x}} 0.9 = 0.0558$$

**2.** Compute: $35 + \sqrt{49}$ =

**3.** What is the probability that one spin of this spinner will result in red?

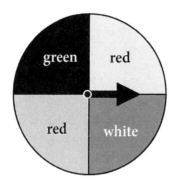

**4.** Fill in the missing numbers.

| y = -2x | | |
|:---:|:---:|:---:|
| **x** | **y** | **(x, y)** |
| -3 | 6 | (-3, 6) |
| -2 | | ( ) |
| | 2 | ( ) |
| 0 | | ( ) |
| 1 | -2 | (1, -2) |
| | -4 | ( ) |
| 3 | | ( ) |

Uh oh, grid lock!

## 5. Challenge Problem

Draw a parachute at the following locations:

(–6, 2)

(–5, 6)

(–7, 0)

(–8, –6)

(–4, –7)

(0, 5)

(3, –3)

(6, –5)

(10, –1)

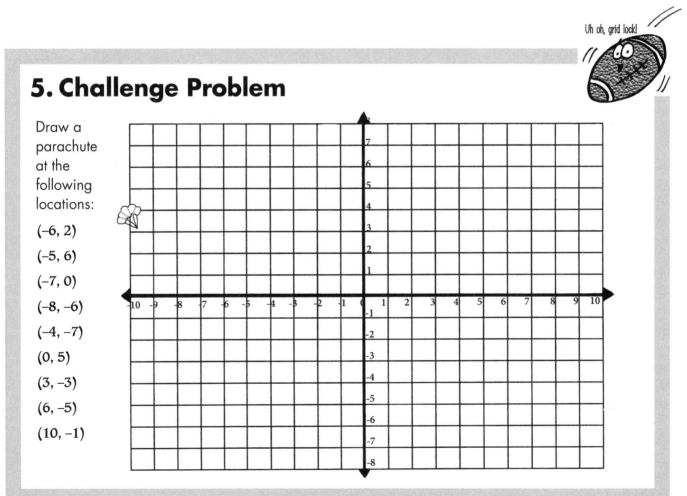

**1.** Compute:  **880 x 405 =**

**2.** Eddie mows 1,764 ft² of lawn in six hours. What is his rate per hour?

**3.** Solve the equation: $2\frac{1}{5}x = 66$

**4.** Which figures are similar to the first one?

a b c d e f g h i

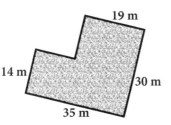

Well, mow me down!

**5.** Hedge-Trimming Competition

Who had the best combined scores?

round 1
round 2

Tom   Tim   Tara   Tess

**1.** Is the computation correct?

**49.07 + 12.92 - 18.003 = 43.987**

**2.** Write an equation and use it to solve the problem.

**Jake pulled 74 weeds in 30 minutes. At this rate, how many weeds will he pull in two hours?**

**3.** Put these in order from greatest to least.

**50,550,005   50,550,050   50,555,000**

**4.** What is the perimeter of this lawn?

19 m
14 m
30 m
35 m

**5.** Use estimation to solve the problem.

**Jake has four lawns of the following dimensions to fertilize.**

72 x 29 feet

40 x 31 feet

48 x 82 feet

48 x 88 feet

**Each bag of fertilizer covers 980 square feet of grass. How many bags will he need to buy?**

Name

**1.** Simplify the expression.

$$8b^9 \div 2b^4 + 12$$

**2.** Natasha plants new grass by scattering handfuls of seeds. Each handful contains 0.79 oz of seed. She scatters a total of 304.94 oz. How many handfuls is this?

**3.** Compute: $9730 \times -40 =$

**4.** Al counts a sampling of the bugs in his yard. Of the 50 bugs he examines, 38 are beetles. If there are 7,500 bugs in the yard, how many could he expect to be beetles?

I have the math bug.

**5.** Which line segments are parallel?

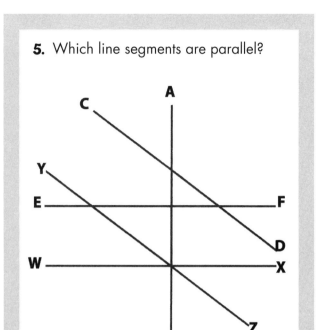

Name

**1.** What number is in the ten millions place?

$$9,463,021,735$$

**2.** Compute: $\frac{1}{2} \times \frac{9}{6} =$

**3.** Solve the equation.

$$12g + 35 = 8g - g$$

**4.** Find the volume of this figure.

10.2 cm
8 cm
6 cm

The answer is in the bag!

**5.** Is this a reasonable calculation?

Seven neighbors rake enough leaves so that they each fill five large bags in one afternoon. A bag holds a volume of 18 cubic feet. All seven of them work for three afternoons. At the end of that time, they calculate that they have raked and bagged 1,900 cubic feet of leaves.

**1.** Is this an accurate solution to the equation?

$$25(d - 4) + d^2 = 164$$
$$d = 8$$

**2.** Show $1\frac{3}{5}$ as a decimal and a percent.

**3.** What property is shown here?

$$5 (10,000 + 13) = (5 \times 10,000) + (5 \times 13)$$

**4.** Write a new problem using the inverse operation. Solve it.

$$98,765 - 56,789 = 41,976$$

## 5. Challenge Problem

Three friends mow these lawns. Who mows the greatest area?

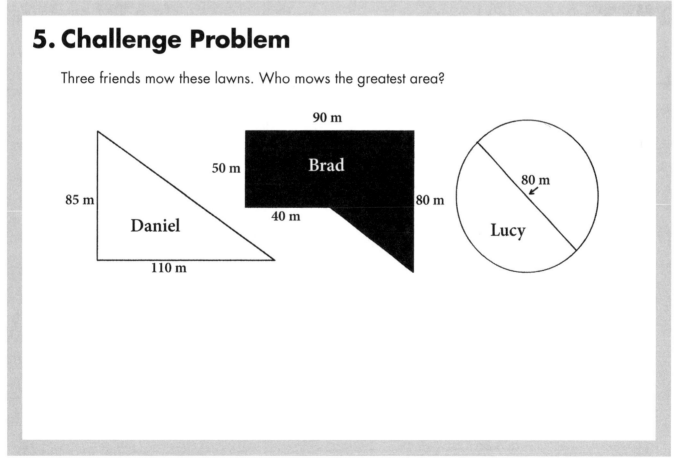

**1.** Compute:   **10,000,000**
                  **– 9,989,898**

**2.** Give a definition of **data**.

**3.** Write an equation that will solve this problem about record-setting food feats, and then solve the problem.

   Rob Williams (USA) made a bologna sandwich with his feet in 103 seconds less time than Danny Healy (UK) ate a raw onion. The sum of their times was 217 seconds. How fast did Danny eat the onion?

**4.** Give two characteristics of a **square**.

Is a square someone who wears plaids and polka dots?

**5.** Some Unusual Eating Records

| Food | Number Eaten | Time (min) |
|---|---|---|
| meatballs | 27 | 1 |
| jam doughnuts | 6 | 3 |
| worms | 94 | 0.5 |
| Brussels sprouts | 43 | 1 |
| cooked sausages | 7 | 1 |

Which food was eaten at the fastest rate?

**1.** The heaviest pumpkin on record weighed 606.7 pounds, if a buyer paid $.68 a pound, find the price to the nearest cent.

**2.** Find q if p = 121.

   **6q – 2q = p + 25**

**3.** A record-setting bean eater ate 226 baked beans (each on a toothpick) in five minutes. How many beans did he eat per minute?

**4.** Round to the nearest ten thousand.

   **1,748,362**

Bean there, done that!

**5.** What formula should be used to find the area of this figure? Write the formula and find the area.

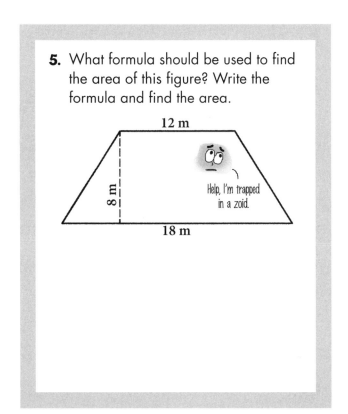

Help, I'm trapped in a zoid.

12 m

8 m

18 m

**1.** Compute:   **–97 – 60 – (–13) =**

**2.** What space figure has four faces?

I'm a space figure.

**3.** Each letter of the alphabet is written on a card and put into a bag. The bag contains only one card for each letter. A girl reaches into the bag and chooses one card. What is the probability that she will not get a vowel?

**4.** Simplify the expression:

$$3\left(\frac{8a}{2}\right)$$

**5.** The world's largest gingerbread man had the dimensions shown in the diagram. Estimate the volume of this record-breaking cookie.

(Assume that the cookie was three inches thick.)

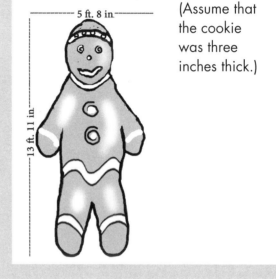

---

**1.** In September 1999, Michael Levinson of Canada set the record for the most grapes stuffed in the mouth. Solve the equation to find how many he held in his mouth at one time.

$$16^2 - 14^2 - g = 6$$

Does that compute?

**2.** Compute: $\frac{6}{6} + \frac{5}{6} =$

**3.** Write this number in standard notation.

**seven hundred million seventy thousand seventy**

**4.** Donald Gorske consumed 18,250 Big Macs between January 1, 1972 and March 7, 2002. How many days did it take to set this record?

**5.** Plot these points on the grid and draw a line to connect them.
(–3, 3) (3, 3) (2, –2) (–2, –2)

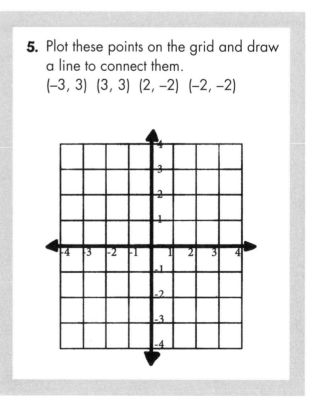

---

**1.** Compute:    **300 x 60,000 =**

**2.** The largest popcorn sculpture in the world was built in the form of King Kong. It was 13 feet tall. This is closest to

a. 300 meters        c. 30 meters

b. 3937 centimeters    d. 300 centimeters

**3.** $b + \frac{c}{4} - 96 = -48$

A. Find b if c = 32.

B. Find b if c = 20.

**4.** Which operation should be done first?

**−86 + (9000 ÷ 25)3**

## 5. Challenge Problem

Read and write Roman numerals to solve these pizza problems.

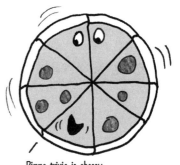

Pizza trivia is cheesy.

a. The longest pizza delivery on record was 6,861 miles. The year of this delivery was MMI. Write the year in standard notation.

b. The largest pizza order was for 13,386 pizzas. The year of this order was MCMXCVIII. Write the year in standard notation.

c. The first pizza dates back to the time of Genghis Kahn. This may be as long ago as the year 1209. Write the year in Roman numerals.

d. The first pizzeria opened in Naples, Italy, in 1830. Write the year in Roman numerals.

e. The first pizzeria in the United States opened in 1895. Write the year in Roman numerals.

**1.** The Greatest Show on Earth Circus Tour of 1890 holds the record for the most performers involved in a circus act. One hundred seventy-five animals and 263 persons took part. Would it be true to say that about 40 percent of the performers were animals?

**2.** Compute: $123 \overline{)56,188}$

Express your answer as a whole number with a remainder.

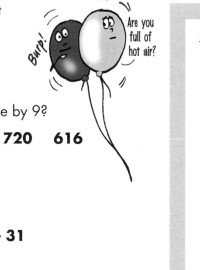

**3.** What is the coefficient of the variable z?

$$6x - 13y + 7z = 34$$

**4.** Draw two similar figures.

**5.** A clown spins the spinner. Find the probability of the outcomes described below.

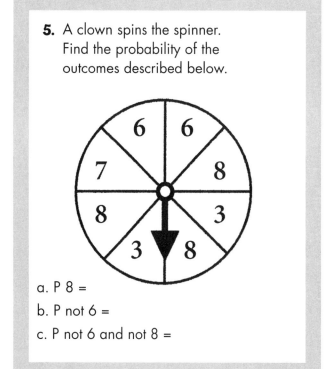

a. P 8 =

b. P not 6 =

c. P not 6 and not 8 =

**1.** The largest travel circus tent has a round top with a 200-foot diameter. What is its circumference?

Burp!

Are you full of hot air?

**2.** Which numbers are divisible by 9?

**3024    9119    404    720    616**

**3.** Simplify the equation.

$$7k + k + 19 = 3k - 31$$

**4.** Compute; round the answer to the nearest tenth:

$$\begin{array}{r} 4.036 \\ \times\ 2.108 \\ \hline \end{array}$$

**5.** Solve this problem.

A circus arena has eight sections of seats, labeled A–H. There are a total of 9,625 seats. Sections A–G have 40 rows of 30 sets in each section. Section H has 35 seats in a row. How many rows of seats are in Section H?

**1.** Compute: $9\overline{)-783}$

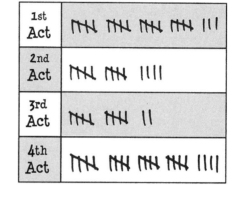

**2.** The heaviest human pyramid on record had 12 people and a weight of 1,700 pounds. What was the average weight per person?

**3.** What values could replace x in the statement?

$$6x + 3 > 2$$

–9    13    7    0    –1    5    –10

**4.** Draw a trapezoid.

**5.** Alan kept this tally sheet of the different number of clown tricks done at a circus performance. What is the total number of tricks?

### Clown Tricks at the Circus

| 1st Act | ̶H̶H̶  ̶H̶H̶  ̶H̶H̶  ̶H̶H̶  III |
|---|---|
| 2nd Act | ̶H̶H̶  ̶H̶H̶  IIII |
| 3rd Act | ̶H̶H̶  ̶H̶H̶  II |
| 4th Act | ̶H̶H̶  ̶H̶H̶  ̶H̶H̶  ̶H̶H̶  IIII |

**1.** Fill in the missing symbol: <, >, or =

$\frac{12}{17}$ ☐ $\frac{5}{8}$

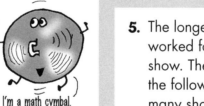

*I'm a math cymbal.*

**2.** Is this pair of numbers (–5, 6) as (s, t) a solution for the equation?

$$\frac{6s}{2} + 7t = 10t - 23$$

**3.** The temperature inside the circus tent rose to 83° F. This is about

28° C        96° C

32° C        54° C

**4.** Compute:

$$\frac{10}{11} \times \frac{10}{12}$$

**5.** The longest-working circus bandmaster worked for 50 years without missing a show. The number of shows he did fits the following characteristics. How many shows in a row did he work?

- 5 digits
- an even number
- divisible by 500
- sum of digits is 5
- 4 digits are the same

**1.** Estimate the number of elephants trained.

| | |
|---|---|
| 4 | number of elephant trainers |
| 32 | number of elephants each trainer has trained each year |
| 13 | number of years each trainer has worked |

**2.** Compute:  $80^9 \div 20^6 =$

**3.** Solve the equation.

$$x - \tfrac{1}{2}x + 5 - 3 = 0$$

**4.** Which angles are congruent?

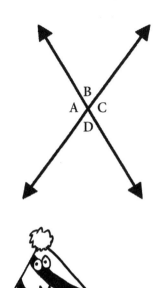

Everybody has an angle.

## 5. Challenge Problem

Finish the pattern by drawing the next three figures.

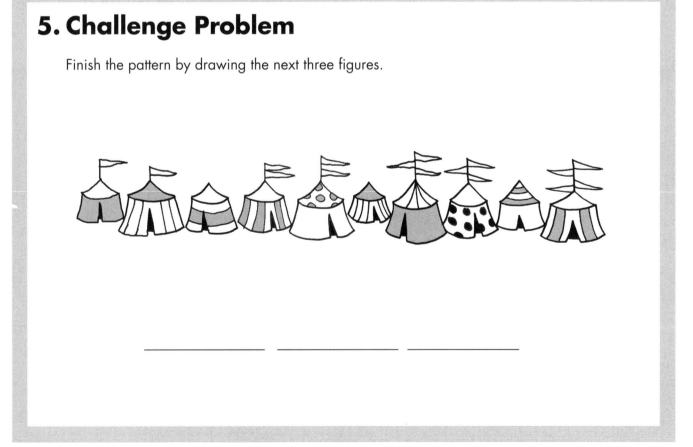

_____   _____   _____

**1.** Compute: **35,555 x 22 =**

**2.** Use mental math to solve the problem.

Mike West (USA) holds the record for the most telephone directories torn in three minutes. He tore 30 phone directories each with 1,052 pages. How many pages did he tear?

**3.** Simplify the equation.

$5(2x - 2) - 3 = 4(x - 3) + 11$

**4.** A weightlifter has barbells of four weights: 30 lb, 50 lb, 70 lb, and 100 lb. She wants to take two on a trip. How many different **combinations** of two are possible?

**5.** Find the symmetrical figures below. For each one, draw at least one line of symmetry. Tell how many lines of symmetry are possible.

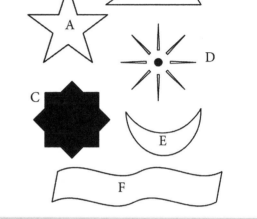

**1.** Write a proportion to solve the problem.

Mark has sprained a wrist or ankle three times out of the last 24 times at the gym. At this rate, how many visits to the gym will it take before he has 12 sprains?

**2.** Solve to find **s** if **t** = −6.

$$\frac{3t}{9} - 10 = s + 5$$

**3.** Sue has won half as many medals as Archie. Archie has won two thirds as many as Georgia. Georgia has won 81. How many has Sue won?

**4.** Compute: **94 ÷ 17.06 =**

**5.** Compare the figures. Which has the greater volume? Which has the greater surface area?

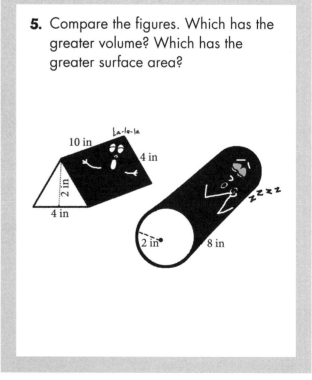

**1.** Compute:     –300 – (–63) + 124 – 66 =

○ –179          ○ 421          ○ –295

○ 179           ○ 295          ○ –421

**2.** Use words to write this expression.

$$6n^2 + 2n + 4$$

**3.** Give the range of this set of data:

| | | | |
|---|---|---|---|
| 6.5 | 9.8 | 3.2 | 1.6 |
| 10.7 | 88.8 | 210 | 66.6 |
| 29.2 | 46.9 | 80 | 31.5 |

**4.** Is this figure a rhombus?

**5.** Solve the problem. Tell how you reached your solution.

**Paddy Doyle (UK) set the world record for the most one-arm pushups by doing 8,794 pushups in five hours. Roy Burger (Canada) set the record for the most regular pushups done in one minute. He did 138.**

What is the difference in their rate of pushups per minute? (Round to the nearest hundredth.)

What's a rhom?

**1.** Write these fractions in lowest terms.

a. $\frac{17}{51}$          b. $\frac{12}{5}$          c. $\frac{18}{360}$

**2.** A map scale is 1 inch = 30 miles. How much real distance is represented by a distance of $4\frac{1}{2}$ inches on the map?

**3.** Solve the equation:

**(n + 70) ÷ 6 = 18**

**4.** Compute: $2\frac{1}{2} \div 1\frac{2}{3} =$

**5.** How much weight was balanced on someone's head?

**The sum of weight lifted or balanced by three amazing feats of strength is 476.5 kg. The greatest weight lifted by teeth is 281.5 kg. The greatest weight lifted by a human beard is 6.3 kg. The greatest weight balanced on a human head is the third feat.**

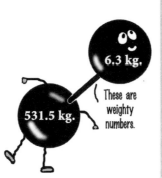

6.3 kg.

531.5 kg.

These are weighty numbers.

**1.** Is the following solution correct?

$\frac{6}{9} \times 5\frac{3}{8} = 3\frac{7}{12}$

**2.** Write a definition of **integers**.

**3.** Compute: **(75 × 13) ÷ 2.5 =**

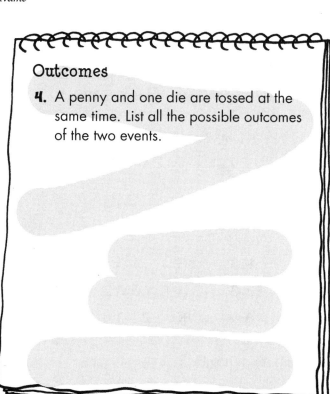

### Outcomes

**4.** A penny and one die are tossed at the same time. List all the possible outcomes of the two events.

# 5. Challenge Problem

Mark Breyden of Australia is the world champion climber of 80-foot poles. He won this record by climbing an 80-foot pole in 9.61 seconds.

Other climbers are practicing and timing their pole-climbing skills.

In one minute, climber Brad climbed 18 feet less than Chad. Tad climbed 7 feet more than Chad. The three climbers climbed 160 feet in one minute.

Which equation will give a value of x that tells how many feet Brad climbed?

   a. **x + (x − 18) + x + 78) = 160**

   b. **x + (x + 18) + (x + 18 + 7) = 160**

   c. **x + (x − 7) + (x − 18 − 7) = 160**

How far did Brad climb?

**1.** How many congruent angles are found in a **scalene triangle**?

Ouch!

**2.** The evening temperature was 13°C. Overnight the temperature fell to –5°C. What is the difference between the two temperatures?

**3.** Compute: **40,000,000 ÷ 800 =**

**4.** A bag contains five grape, seven lime, three cherry, six lemon, and four root beer lollipops. Someone reaches in and gets a cherry lollipop. What is the probability that the second one picked will be root beer?

**5.** Solve the problem. Tell how you solved it.

> A team of volunteer doctors traveled to 18 countries, performing surgeries on 5,139 patients. This medical tour lasted from February 5 to April 14, 1999.

a. What was the average number of surgeries performed per country?

b. What was the average number of surgeries performed per day?

**1.** Use the inverse operation to verify the accuracy of the computation.

**65.032 – 39.4706 = 25.5614**

Here's another tricky math operation.

**2.** Solve the equation.

**8x – 4 = 10 + 4x**

**3.** Which of the following are irrational numbers?

a. $\frac{5}{6}$    d. –60.333...
c. 0.37    e. 0.454454454...
b. 0.37    f. –92.32

**4.** Find the volume of this figure.

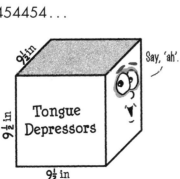

$9\frac{1}{2}$ in

$9\frac{1}{2}$ in

Tongue Depressors

Say, 'ah'.

$9\frac{1}{2}$ in

**5.** Tell what information is missing that would make this a problem that can be solved.

> Balamurati Ambasti is the youngest physician on record. He graduated from medical school on May 19, 1995. How old was he when he graduated?

**1.** Compute: $-9.4\overline{\smash{)}830.02}$

**2.** Which kind of graph would you use to show the number and kinds of surgeries performed at a hospital in one day?

bar graph        double bar graph

circle graph     pictograph

line graph       double line graph

**3.** **(96 x −3) x 40 =**

**4.** Charles Jensen, from South Dakota, has had the most operations of anyone on record. He had 970 operations from the end of July, 1954 to the end of 1994. What was the rate of operations per month?

**5.** Name the transformations shown here.

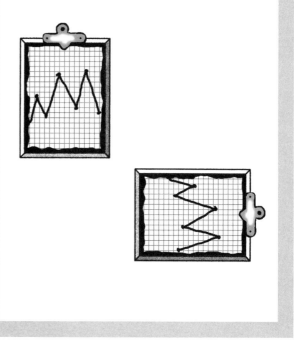

**1.** Which operation should be done first?

$9(680 \div 40) + 6x^2 = 89$

**2.** Which fractions are equivalent to $\frac{4}{6}$?

$\frac{17}{22}$        $\frac{2}{3}$        $\frac{6}{9}$

$\frac{98}{147}$       $\frac{7}{9}$        $\frac{42}{63}$

I'm a fractured fraction.

**3.** Compute: $20\frac{1}{10} - 7\frac{3}{10} =$

**4.** The highest body temperature ever recorded was 115.5°F. Convert this temperature to Celsius.

**5.** The country of Monaco has one doctor for every 169 people. The country of Malawi has one doctor for every 49,118 people.

a. Write a ratio that compares the number of people per doctor in Malawi to the number in Monaco.

b. Write the ratio as a percent. (Round to the nearest whole percent.)

**1.** Which example shows the **associative property**?

a. **3(9 x 4.3) = (3 x 9) + (3 x 4.3)**

b. **0.05 + 7.2.9 = 72.9 + 0.25**

c. **9730 x 1 = 1 x 8730**

d. **(63 + x²) + 90 = 63 + (x² + 90)**

**3.** Simplify the expression.

**(3y – 2)y**

**4.** Use words to write this expression.

$\sqrt{256} - 7(s + 6)$

**2.** Fill in the missing operation.

$\sqrt{196}$ ☐ $\frac{7}{8}$ = $12\frac{1}{4}$

It's time for a do-over.

scratch scratch

# 5. Challenge Problem

After two friends read about a man who hiccuped for 684 days and a woman who sneezed for a total of 978 days, they started counting their hiccups and sneezes. The table shows the data they collected. Show this data in a double line graph.

## Hiccups and Sneezes 2005

| Month | Hiccups | Sneezes |
|-------|---------|---------|
| Jan | 100 | 200 |
| Feb | 140 | 300 |
| Mar | 210 | 260 |
| Apr | 250 | 300 |
| May | 300 | 110 |
| Jun | 270 | 210 |
| July | 320 | 180 |
| Aug | 150 | 240 |
| Sept | 280 | 150 |
| Oct | 350 | 220 |
| Nov | 190 | 290 |
| Dec | 200 | 160 |

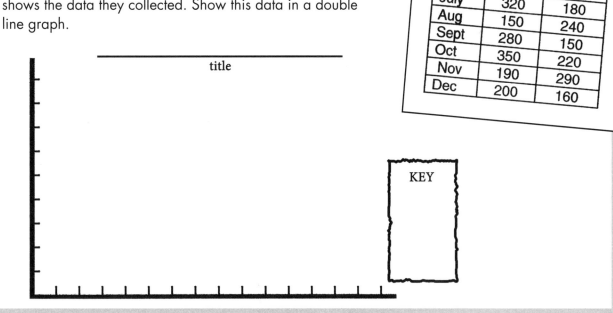

title

KEY

**1.** Brooke wants to buy this sale item. Name the shape of this figure.

**2.** Simplify the equation.

**93k – 82 = 100k + 50**

**3.** Compute:     228,172
               – 33,846

**4.** The most expensive baseball glove (Lou Gehrig's) sold at an auction for **$389,500**. The most valuable hair clippings (Elvis Presley's) went for **$115,120**. The most expensive bikini (covered with diamonds) cost **$194,458.97**. What would it cost to buy all three?

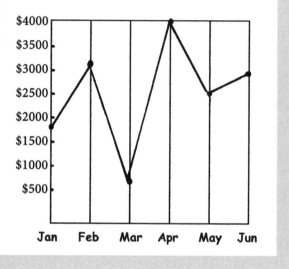

**5. Money Sam Spent at Auctions January – June 2004**

What is the range of the amounts of money Sam spent over the six months?

**1.** Compute:     $9.009 \overline{)3603.6}$

**2.** Moe calculated that the capacity of his shopping bag was 5,000 square inches. Is this a reasonable measurement?

**3.** Is this a correct graph of the statement?

**x > –2**

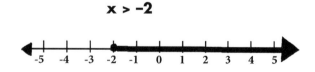

**4.** Suzie bought five drums and six tambourines at a big sale. What is the ratio of drums to the number of instruments she bought?

**5.** Ramon went to the big guitar sale with $700.00. He chose a guitar with an original price of $830. The store added six percent sales tax to the sale price. Did he have enough money to buy the guitar?

Year-End
Guitar Sale

20% Off
All
Guitars

**1.** There is a box containing ten $20 bills, three $50 bills, and two $100 bills. If you grab two bills, what is the probability you will get two $100s?

*Imagine that!*

**2.** Compute: **7050 – (–7050) =**

**3.** Nine U.S. currency bills total $77. What could these be?

**4.** Which angle is **supplementary** to Angle ABD?

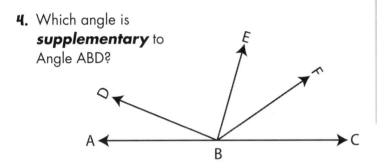

**5.** The most valuable guitar on record was Jerry Garcia's "Tiger" guitar. It sold at an auction for $957,500.00. This amount is $42,500.00 less than 2,000 times what my neighbor Al paid for his new guitar.

Would any of the following equations determine what Al paid for his guitar?

a. $2{,}000x = \$957{,}500.00 - \$42{,}500.00$

b. $\frac{1}{2{,}000}x = \$957{,}500.00 + \$42{,}500.00$

c. $2{,}000x + \$42{,}500.00 = \$957{,}500.00$

d. $2{,}000x - \$42{,}400.00 = \$957{,}500.00$

**1.** Write an equation with integers to find the amount of money Zack gave Zoey.

**On Saturday, Zack borrowed $394.00 from Zoey. By Friday, Zack had given Zoey enough money that she had an extra $117.00.**

*Feed me!*

**2.** Compute: $\frac{4}{5} \times \frac{7}{8} =$

**3.** Circle the units that can measure capacity.

| | | | |
|---|---|---|---|
| quart | decade | gram | milliliter |
| degree | gallon | decimeter | cubic centimeter |
| liter | pint | kilogram | square meter |

**4.** Fill in the missing sign: <, >, or =

**8.0909** ☐ **8.09909**

**5.** Finish the table to show the ordered pairs for this equation.

| x= -4y | | |
|---|---|---|
| **x** | **y** | **(x, y)** |
| **-16** | | ( ) |
| | 2 | ( ) |
| **0** | | ( ) |
| **8** | | ( ) |
| | -1 | ( ) |

**1.** These are the amounts of money Aunt Charlene spent each day last week at the mall. What was the average amount she spent per day?

| $ 63.25 | Mon |
|---|---|
| 82.18 | Tue |
| 40.80 | Wed |
| 137.10 | Thurs |
| 99.22 | Fri |

**2.** Is this correct?

$$\sqrt{144} = 6^2 - 4^2 - 2^3$$

**3.** Solve the equation.

$$n + (n + 1) + (n + 2) = -87$$

**4.** Which operation should be done first?

$$\$498.00 - \$26.50 - 4(\$0.10 + \$18.00) =$$

## 5. Challenge Problem

The world's most valuable book is an original set of J. J. Audubon's *The Birds of America*. It was sold at an auction in New York City in March 2000, for $8,802,500.00.

Assume the purchase was paid in cash and that the buyer had bills in only these denominations: $10, $20, and $50. Find three different combinations of the three kinds of bills that could have been used to pay for the book set.

BIGGEST BIRD BOOK EVER!

This book is not 'cheep'.

**1.** How many different **permutations** are possible for five friends waiting in line to buy tickets for a swim meet?

Give me five!

**2.** Compute:  $16\overline{\smash{\big)}15{,}984}$

**3.** The deepest recorded dive by a turtle is 3,937 feet. The deepest recorded free dive by a human is 656 feet. What is the difference?

**4.** Solve the equation.

$\frac{n}{8} - 12 = 11\frac{1}{2}$

**5.** Name the line that represents the intersection of Plane ABCD and Plane EFGH.

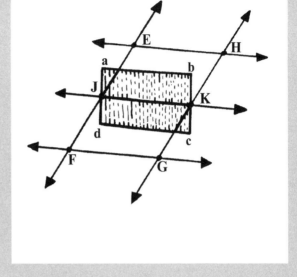

**1.** What unit of measure is appropriate to measure the depth of a large city swimming pool for adult swimmers?

○ millimeters  ○ kilometers  ○ liters  ○ feet

○ milliliters  ○ grams  ○ gallons  ○ inches

**2.** Solve the equation.

**−17d = 11.05**

**3.** The longest ocean swim was 197 k. The longest white water swim was 184.93 k shorter. Compute the difference.

Dive right in!

**4.** Round to the nearest thousandth:

**12.56793**

**5.** What conclusion can you draw about the speed of the different strokes?

**Swimming Records**

| Event | Time (sec) |
|---|---|
| Women 50-m freestyle | 23.59 |
| Women 50-m backstroke | 26.83 |
| Women 50-m butterfly | 25.36 |
| Women 50-m breaststroke | 29.96 |
| Men 50-m freestyle | 21.13 |
| Men 50-m backstroke | 23.31 |
| Men 50-m butterfly | 22.74 |
| Men 50-m breaststroke | 26.20 |

**1.** Compute:   **−1022 ÷ (−14) =**

**2.** Identify this figure.

**3.** Find z if w is −9.

$$\frac{6w}{9} - z + 12 = -5$$

**4.** Is 14,000 a good estimate for the solution to this problem?

**9 (724 + 885) − 988 =**

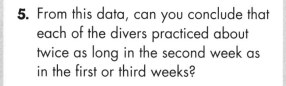

**5.** From this data, can you conclude that each of the divers practiced about twice as long in the second week as in the first or third weeks?

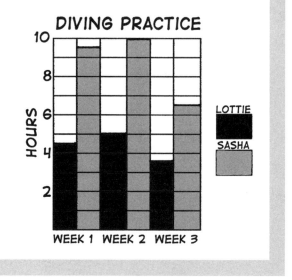

DIVING PRACTICE

LOTTIE
SASHA

**1.** Change the fraction to a decimal. (Round to the nearest one hundredth.)   $\frac{11}{12}$

**2.** Draw the graph of this number sentence.

**x ≤ 3**

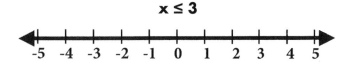

**3.** Compute:   $\frac{3}{4} \div \frac{3}{4}$

**4.** Ragnhild Hveger of Denmark set 42 world swimming records from 1936 to 1942. What was the average number she set in each year?

**5.** Find the area of this figure.

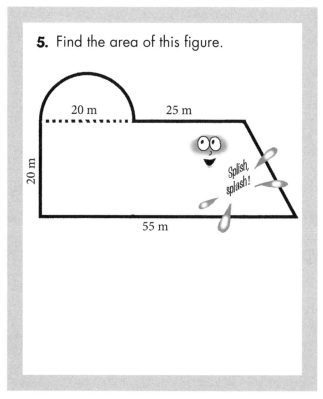

20 m     25 m

20 m

55 m

*Splish, splash!*

**1.** Which equation will help find the solution to this problem?

In June, Ralph practiced nine hours more than in July and twice as long as in May. He practiced a total of 391 hours in the three months. How long did Ralph practice in July?

___ a. $t + \frac{t}{2} + (t + 9) = 391$

___ b. $t + \frac{t}{2} + (t - 9) = 391$

___ c. $2t + t + (t + 9) = 391$

___ d. $381 - 2t + t + 9$

**2.** A swimmer's clothing, goggles, and towel weigh 3.75 pounds. How many ounces is this?

**3.** Compute:

**256 – 63 =**

**4.** Correct the mistakes.

```
   116
  1209
    82
   161
    99
 + 235
 2,802
```

Don't tell me...
Don't tell me...

---

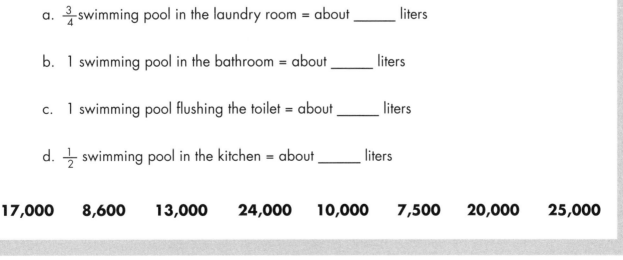

## 5. Challenge Problem

A report about water uses in Australian homes found that each year the average household in Melbourne used close to three times the amount of water found in an average home swimming pool. This amounts to about 52,000 liters per year.

Look at the findings of the study about places the water is used. Use mental math to estimate the number of liters used in each location. Choose the closest amount from the numbers below.

a. $\frac{3}{4}$ swimming pool in the laundry room = about _____ liters

b. 1 swimming pool in the bathroom = about _____ liters

c. 1 swimming pool flushing the toilet = about _____ liters

d. $\frac{1}{2}$ swimming pool in the kitchen = about _____ liters

**17,000     8,600     13,000     24,000     10,000     7,500     20,000     25,000**

**1.** Which of these are real numbers?

○ **225**  ○ **70⁵**  ○ **7.26432 …**

○ $\frac{3}{9}$  ○ **2$\frac{1}{2}$**  ○ **10.09**

○ **6.555**  ○ **–72**  ○ **15.3**

**2.** A maypole was 48 feet tall after three 4-foot sections were sawed off. Write and solve an equation that will find the original height.

**3.** Compute: **123 x 456 =**

**4.** Draw a triangular prism.

**5.** Solve the problem. Tell how you solved it.

> **Walker school created a maypole for a May Day festival. The maypole has 40 ribbons: 12 blue, 9 pink, 10 yellow, and the rest white. A child grabs one ribbon at random. What are the odds against it being pink or white?**

My daddy was a maypole.

**1.** Solve.

**–g + 30 – (2g + g) =**

**2.** A kilogram is closest to

○ 5 pounds   ○ 1 meter   ○ 10 grams

○ 3 yards   ○ $\frac{1}{2}$ mile   ○ 2 pounds

○ 1 pound   ○ 2 ounces   ○ 100,000 grams

**3.** Compute: **400.4 x 1.6 =**

i'm having a party.

**4.** Al has 80 quarters and 60 dimes. Sal has 380 nickels and 10 dimes. Val has 5 quarters, 130 dimes, and 500 pennies. Who has the most money?

**5.** The world's largest bonfire was built in 2003 for a celebration in Japan. It was stacked in the general shape of a rectangular prism with a height of 123 feet and a base area of 86 square feet. What formula should be used to find the volume of the bonfire? What is the volume of the bonfire?

62

**1.** Fill in the blank with the correct term:

_____ **is a method of estimating or predicting an approximate number of events that will occur among a very large set of items.**

**2.** Compute:  **−37 + 66 + (−7) =**

**3.** Write an equation that will help you solve this problem.

**At an Easter egg hunt, there were a total of 4,680 eggs hidden. The number of real eggs was two-thirds the number of chocolate eggs. How many eggs were chocolate?**

**4.** How many vertices are found on a sphere?

**5.** The largest pumpkin-carving event took place on the set of the CBS TV Early Show on October 31, 2002. Steven Clarke carved 42 pumpkins in one hour. At this rate, how many pumpkins could he carve . . .

___ a. in 45 minutes?

___ b. in $4\frac{1}{2}$ hours?

___ c. from 8:20 am to 11:15 am?

*Easter is my favorite holiday.*

**1.** Circle the prime numbers.

**3   7   9   23   29   33   47   57**

**2.** At the world's largest Camel Wrestling Festival in 1994, 20,000 people watched 120 camels wrestle. Write a ratio that compares the number of people to camels. (Reduce to lowest terms.)

**3.** Compute:  **25 − $6\frac{7}{8}$ =**

**4.** Is this solution correct?

**96n ÷ (17 − 13) = −144**
**n = −4**

*i'm all tied up!*

**5.** In 2002, the world's largest ribbon-cutting ceremony was attended by 3,238 participants. The ribbon was 13,789 feet long.

If the ribbon was 0.25 feet (three inches wide), what was its perimeter?

*Name*

**1.** Compute:  **(9 x 38) ÷ 4 =**

**2.** Find p if q is 25.

$$16q - 30 + p^2 = 491$$

**3.** Estimate the answer.

**35,887 x 609 =**

**4.** At the largest monkey buffet in the world, 2,000 monkeys ate 660 pounds of fruits and vegetables. Assume one monkey reached into a pile of mixed fruit that contained 1,200 oranges, 600 pears, and 800 apples. If this was done without looking or trying for a particular fruit, what is the probability that the monkey will get an orange?

cha-cha-cha!

I wasn't invited to the party.

## 5. Challenge Problem

Examine the angles in the figure. Write T (true) or F(false) for each statement about the angles.

___ a. Angles 3 and 6 are alternate interior angles.

___ b. Angles 1 and 7 are alternate exterior angles.

___ c. Angles 1 and 5 are corresponding angles.

___ d. Angles 4 and 5 are alternate interior angles.

___ e. Angles 2 and 7 are alternate exterior angles.

___ f. Angles 6 and 7 are corresponding angles.

___ g. Angles 1 and 6 are alternate exterior angles.

___ h. Angles 3 and 5 are alternate interior angles.

Explain your answer.

**1.** Compute:   123,456,789
            + 987,654,321

**2.** The name of a month is drawn from a bag that has the name of each month written only once. What are the odds in favor of getting a month that does not begin with the letter J?

**3.** Write the words to match the expression.

$$a - 2b^2$$

**4.** Use trial and error to find the number of bees described below.

In 1990, a pair of magicians produced a large number of bees during a TV special. The number is a four-digit, even number. The first digit has the greatest value. Three digits are the same, and the sum of the digits is eight.

**5.** Which angle is congruent to B?

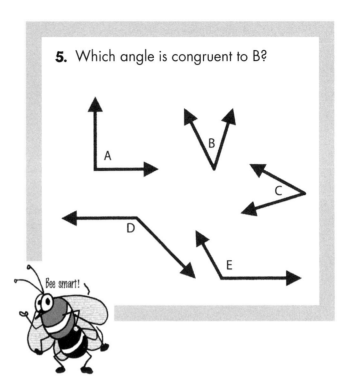

Bee smart!

**1.** Round to the nearest ten thousand.

3,673,425,198

**2.** Simplify the equation.

$$9w^2 + 7w^2 - 10w + 15 = 1485$$

**3.** Compute:   16.35 + 194.762 =

**4.** A horse performs in a circle that has a 12-meter diameter. What is the area of the circle?

**5.** Use mental math to solve the problem.

The oldest snake on record was a boa constrictor named Popeye. The snake died on April 15, 1977 at the age of 40 years, 3 months, and 14 days. When was Popeye born?

The answer is NOT s-s-s-seven.

**1.** Write a mathematical statement to match the words.

The sum of negative forty and sixteen divided by a number (n) is equal to or greater than four.

**2.** Describe how a central angle (in a circle) is formed.

**3.** Compute:     **−300 x (−68) =**

**4.** The heaviest raccoon, Bandit, weighed 64.9 pounds. Some small raccoons weigh between 2.7 percent and 4% of Bandit's weight. Find the range of weights for the smaller raccoons. Round the numbers to the nearest tenth.

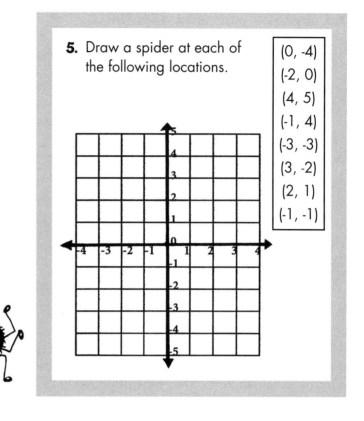

I try not to be negative.

**5.** Draw a spider at each of the following locations.

(0, -4)
(-2, 0)
(4, 5)
(-1, 4)
(-3, -3)
(3, -2)
(2, 1)
(-1, -1)

**1.** Solve the problem. Explain how you solved it. Tell what operations you used.

**The earliest zoo started about 2097 BC. How long ago was this?**

**2.** Compute:     $8\frac{2}{3} \times 6\frac{3}{5} =$

**3.** Solve the equation.

**−11y = 44**

**4.** Write this number in standard notation.

**six hundred sixty thousand sixteen**

Keep me away from those elephants.

**5.** The largest animal orchestra was made up of 12 elephants playing percussion instruments. The orchestra might have played in an arena of this shape. What is the perimeter of this arena?

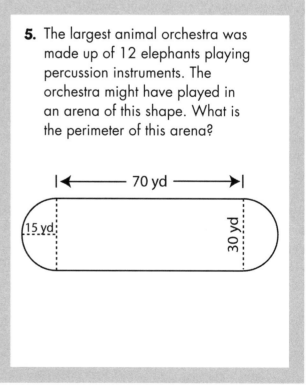

70 yd

15 yd          30 yd

**1.** Use the inverse operation to check the accuracy of the answer. Show your work.

$$86{,}520 \div 20 = 4326$$

**3.** Compute:
$$\begin{array}{r} 500 \\ \times\ 90 \\ \hline \end{array}$$

**4.** A girl draws a letter of the alphabet from a basket and tosses a penny to see how it lands. The probability of her getting the letter P and heads on the penny is 1/52. Give the definition of independent events. Then tell if these are independent events (drawing the letter and tossing the penny).

**2.** Which ordered pairs (x, y) are solutions to the equation y = –x + 4?

- ○ a. (7, –3)
- ○ b. (–2, 6)
- ○ c. (0, 4)
- ○ d. (–3, –7)

I keep landing on my head!

Hey, that's my job!

---

## 5. Challenge Problem

Some of the fastest animals on Earth can cover amazing distances. These estimated distances assume that the animal keeps moving consistently at their record speed.

**The fastest kangaroo could cover 70 miles in one hour and 45 minutes.**
**The fastest land animal (the cheetah) could cover 31 miles in one-half hour.**
**The fastest bird in level flight (the red-breasted merganser) could cover 118 miles in two hours and twenty minutes.**

a. What rate can each of the three animals travel (in miles per hour)?

_____

b. What is the difference in rate from the fastest to the second fastest?

_____

**1.** Write an equation to match the statement.

**Twelve less than a negative number (b) is half the sum of eighteen and fourteen**

**2.** Compute:    5 )‾273,608‾

**3.** The longest taxi ride was 21,691 miles and cost $63,500. What was the cost per mile?

(Round your answer to the nearest cent)

**4.** The number of edges on a pentagonal pyramid is

  **6      10      8      5      12**

**5.** Two friends took a long trip on a lawnmower. The graph shows how they spent their time during each 24-hour period. Estimate the amount of time they spent sleeping each day.

*See you next spring.*

**1.** Compute:    **1170.75 ÷ 176 =**

**2.** The longest trip by pedal boat covered 7500 kilometers. A man from Kobe, Japan pedaled from October 30, 1992 to February 17, 1993. How long was the trip (in days)?

*Leapfrog, anyone?*

**3.** Write this number in expanded notation.

  **6,300,925**

**4.** What number is the opposite of **100.001?**

**5.** Write an equation that will solve this problem, then solve it.

**Some friends took an unusual ten-day trip, leapfrogging across their state for 996 miles. They traveled the same distance on each of the first eight days. On day 9, they traveled 35 fewer miles than on days 1-8. On day 10, they traveled 18 fewer miles than days 1-8. How far did they travel on day 5?**

(Round your answer to the nearest mile.)

**1.** Which operation should be done second?

$$5(11n) - n + 14 =$$

**2.** Solve the problem. Tell how you solved it.

Lucy started an inner tube trip on Saturday, October 22, at 9:00 am. She traveled 156 miles at a rate of 1.5 miles an hour. When did she finish the trip?

**3.** Compute:

$$-99 \overline{)9801}$$

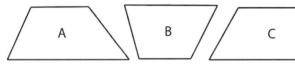
Don't push me.

**4.** Which figure is an isosceles trapezoid?

A    B    C

**5.** Which journey took place at a rate of about 4.1 miles per hour?

### SOME INTERESTING JOURNEYS

| Journey | distance (miles) | Time (hours) |
|---|---|---|
| leapfrogging | 996 | 245 |
| paddling an inner tube | 210 | 122 |
| pushing a bed | 3024 | 432 |
| riding a lawnmower | 7600 | 190 |

**1.** Which is greater? $12^6$ or $8^9$

**2.** Solve the equation.

$$10a^2 + 39 = 9a^2 + 48$$

**3.** Compute:    $\frac{3}{8} \div \frac{2}{3} =$

Race your bathtub and get clean, too.

**4.** Gonzo's bathtub is 126 cm long, 49 cm wide, and 73 cm deep. He estimates that the volume is about 48,000 cubic centimeters. Is this a reasonable measurement?

**5.** Create a table to help solve this problem.

In a 2005 bathtub race, the team from Tampa had 48 participants. There were 35 from Boise, 25 from Seattle, 21 from Boston, and 43 from San Diego. In the 2004 race, there were 29 participants from Boston, San Diego, Seattle, Boise, and Tampa.

What is the difference in participation for each city?

What is the difference in total participation between the two years?

**1.** Write a number sentence that shows the ***identity property for addition.***

**3.** Compute:

$$\begin{array}{r} 9{,}000{,}900 \\ -\ 8{,}765{,}432 \end{array}$$

**2.** Find a pair of numbers (x, y) that makes this statement true.

$$\frac{2y}{x} = -4$$

**4.** Bob flips a coin. Rob draws the name of one weekday from a bag that has one slip of paper for each day of the week. What is the probability of tails and a day not beginning with T or S?

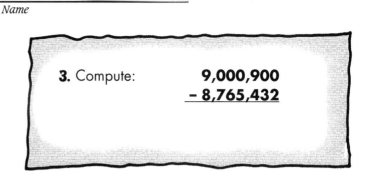

I'm beating a pair of crutches.

# 5. Challenge Problem

Find the average distance of these record-setting journeys.

*(Round the answer to the nearest whole mile.)*

| | |
|---|---|
| longest treadmill walk in 24 hours | 116.04 miles |
| longest distance on a waterslide in 24 hours | 420.652 miles |
| longest bathtub sail in 24 hours | 90.5 miles |
| longest backward walk in 24 hours | 95.4 miles |
| longest wheelchair journey in 24 hours | 112.5 miles |

Do you have more time? Find the rate (in miles per hour) for each feat.

**1.** It takes $11\frac{9}{10}$ Earth years for Jupiter to revolve around the Sun once. This is $17\frac{4}{8}$ fewer years than Saturn's revolution time. How long does it take Saturn to make the trip?

*(Write the answer as a decimal.)*

**2.** Are the terms like or unlike?

$3z^2 + 5z^3 - 7z$

**3.** Earth is 93 million miles from the Sun. Neptune is 2.8 billion miles from the Sun.

Compute the difference.

**4.** Name this figure.

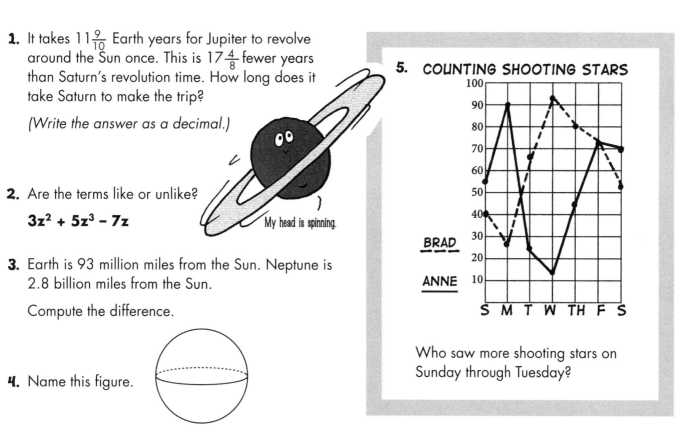

**5. COUNTING SHOOTING STARS**

BRAD

ANNE

Who saw more shooting stars on Sunday through Tuesday?

**1.** Write this number in standard notation.

**ninety and thirteen seventeenths**

**2.** Describe the pattern. Fill in the missing number to fit the pattern.

**8,016,734; 4,801,673; _____; 7,348,016**

**3.** Compute:  **3.02 x 7.51**

**4.** Find the difference between the volume of the two figures. Round to the nearest whole centimeter.

40 cm   30 cm   20 cm   10 cm   25 cm   25 cm

**5.** Tell what operations are needed to solve the problem, and in what order you would use them.

**The largest meteorite hit the Earth in Namibia. It weighs 60 metric tons. This is 15 tons less than twice the weight of nine large buses. What is the weight of each bus?**

Let me jot this down.

*Name*

**1.** Compute: **– 4000 – 40 – (–4) =**

**2.** Draw the name of a planet from a box that has each planet's name one time. Choose the name of a month from another box that has the name of each month one time. How many different outcomes are possible for these two events?

**3.** Simplify the equation.

**36y – 14 = 90 + 10y**

**4.** Describe the measurement of the angles in a right triangle.

### 5. Moons for the Nine Planets

Wow!

| Planets | # of Moons |
|---------|-----------|
| Mercury | 0 |
| Venus | 0 |
| Earth | 1 |
| Mars | 2 |
| Neptune | 8 |
| Saturn | 18 |
| Jupiter | 16 |
| Uranus | 15 |
| Pluto | 1 |

Andrea has calculated that 6.7 is the average number of moons for the nine planets. Is her calculation correct?

*Name*

**1.** Round to the nearest ten.

$$168 \frac{7}{10}$$

**2.** The average temperature on the planet Pluto is 380°F. Give the formula that can be used to convert this into a Celsius temperature. Then find the Celsius temperature.

**3.** Compute: $\frac{7}{12} - \frac{5}{9} =$

**4.** Solve the equation.

**3b ÷ 40 = –100**

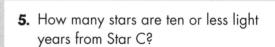

**5.** How many stars are ten or less light years from Star C?

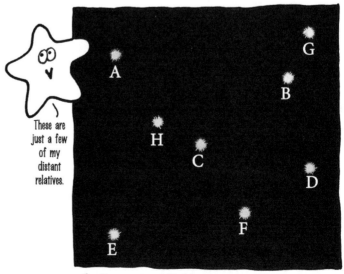

These are just a few of my distant relatives.

Scale: 1 cm = 4 light years

72

**1.** Uranus is $1.8 \times 10^9$ miles from the Sun.

Mars is $1.42 \times 10^8$ miles from the Sun

Compute the answer in scientific notation. Explain how you solved the problem. What is the difference in their distance from the sun?

**2.** 250 is 40 percent of what number?

**3.** Solve the equation.

$$-34b = 71.74$$

**4.** Find the mistakes and give the correct answer.

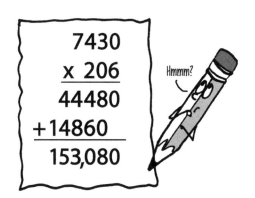

```
  7430
x  206
 44480
+14860
153,080
```

Hmmm?

---

## 5. Challenge Problem

The table shows how the surface gravity on other planets relates to the strength of gravity on Earth. An astronaut weighs 200 pounds on Earth. Calculate what his weight would be on each of the other planets.

A. astronaut's weight on Mercury =

B. astronaut's weight on Venus =

C. astronaut's weight on Mars =

D. astronaut's weight on Jupiter =

E. astronaut's weight on Saturn =

F. astronaut's weight on Uranus =

G. astronaut's weight on Neptune =

H. astronaut's weight on Pluto =

Earth is the universal standard.

### SURFACE GRAVITY ON THE NINE PLANETS

| | |
|---|---|
| Earth | 1 |
| Mercury | Earth x 0.38 |
| Venus | Earth x 0.9 |
| Mars | Earth x 0.38 |
| Jupiter | Earth x 2.7 |
| Saturn | Earth x 1.2 |
| Uranus | Earth x 0.93 |
| Neptune | Earth x 1.5 |
| Pluto | Earth x 0.03 |

*Name*

**1.** The world's longest hot dog measured 122 ft, 8 in. The world's largest salami measured 498 ft, 3.6 in. How much longer was the salami?

**2.** Which operation should be done first?

$$95(30 - 17) + 72 =$$

**3.** A picnic basket is filled with sandwiches: 12 ham and 4 turkey, all wrapped in plain paper. Pat takes two sandwiches, one at a time. What is the probability that she will get one of each kind of sandwich?

**5.** Does this show a graph of x = -y?

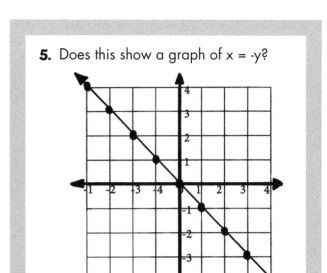

**4.** Which figures are similar to A?

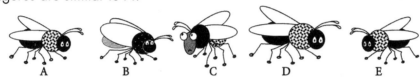

A    B    C    D    E

*Name*

**1.** Which places have a zero value in this number?

**903,100,610**

**2.** An average soda pop can holds $1\frac{1}{2}$ cups of soda. The average soda pop consumption in the U.S. in 2003 was 51.7 gallons per person. About how many cans is this per person?

○ 225     ○ 550     ○ 100

○ 55     ○ 100     ○ 5,000

**3.** Compute:    **$1737.00 ÷ 18 =**

**4.** Solve the equation: **−9a = 24 + a**

**5.**

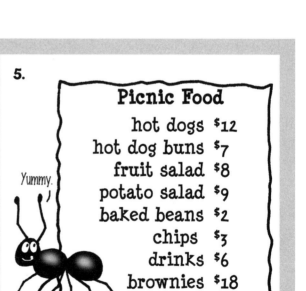

**Picnic Food**

hot dogs $12
hot dog buns $7
fruit salad $8
potato salad $9
baked beans $2
chips $3
drinks $6
brownies $18
watermelon $5

Yummy.

Find the cost of the picnic food bill with a 6.5 percent tax added.

**1.** Compute: **– 17 + 23 + (–16) + (–7) =**

**2.** Find the **median** of these prices.

**$20   $18   $47   $33   $12   $55   $9**

**3.** Fill in the missing symbol >, <, or =. Assume x is not equal to 0.

**–17 + 2x** ☐ **–17 + 2x²**

**4.** Draw a cylinder. Tell which of the following are true of a cylinder.

    a. has two edges

    b. has only two faces

    c. has no vertices

    d. has one rectangular face

*Chow time!*

**5.** Use the grid to draw a picnic tablecloth that has these corners:

(

**1.** Simplify the expression:

$$9p + 13p - 2(p + q) - 15q$$

**2.** People in Ireland are the world's largest consumers of baked beans, eating 197 ounces per person per year. Find the rate of consumption per month (rounded to the nearest pound).

**3.** What is the greatest common factor of 18 and 117?

**4.** Compute: $12 \frac{9}{10} \times 2 \frac{2}{3} =$

*Give me an ...A ...B ...C ...D!*

**5.**

  A. The formula to find the volume of a cone is

    ○ $V = \Pi r^2 h$      ○ $V = \Pi dh$

    ○ $V = \frac{1}{2} \Pi r^2 h$      ○ $V = \frac{1}{3} \Pi r^2 h$

  B. A megaphone has an 8-inch diameter and a 10-inch height. Its volume is closest to

    a. 500 in³

    b. 250 in³

    c. 170 in³

    d. 670 in³

*Name*

**1.** Compute:    **860,000 ÷ 40 =**

    a. 2,150       c. 21,500

    b. 2,100       d. 215,000

**2.** Fill in the missing operation.

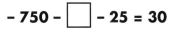

$- 750 - \boxed{\phantom{x}} - 25 = 30$

**3.** Simplify the equation.

$\frac{3}{4}d + \frac{1}{2}d - 70 = \frac{1}{2}d + 5$

**4.** The world's largest picnic was held in 2005 to celebrate the opening of a San Francisco grocery store. Free picnic lunches were given to 500 guests. They were invited to sit on a red and white picnic blanket that had an area of 10,000 square feet. Give three different sets of dimensions that could result in a 10,000-foot square blanket.

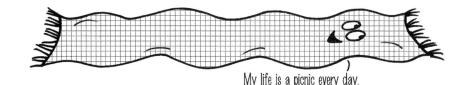

My life is a picnic every day.

# 5. Challenge Problem

Four friends stuffed themselves at a picnic.
Each of them ate too much of a different picnic food.
Draw a diagram of four stick figures in a row.
Label them from left to right: Dan, Sam, Charlie, Brad
Assume the friends were at a long picnic table with others around them.

Use the diagram, the written clues, and good logic to find out who ate the baked beans.

1. Dan ate no cupcakes.

2. Sam ate no potato salad.

3. Brad ate no hot dogs.

4. Charlie ate no hot dogs.

5. The cupcake eater is between the hot dog eater and the potato salad eater.

**Who ate the baked beans?**

**1.** Correct the mistakes.

```
   1,269
   4,034
 + 5,122
  11,415
```

**2.** Mt. Everest, the world's highest mountain, is 29,035 feet tall. The tallest U.S. mountain, Mt. McKinley, is 61,194 meters. Find the difference. Explain how you solved the problem.

**3.** Use words to write the expression. $3(n - 4)$

**4.** This space figure has been cut open. What figure is it?

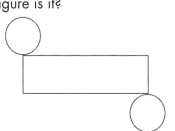

**5.** Find the mean of the heights of the world's six tallest mountains.

## World's Highest Mountains

|   | Name | Height *Feet* |
|---|------|---------------|
| 1 | Everest | 29,035 |
| 2 | K2 | 28,238 |
| 3 | Kangchenjunga | 28,208 |
| 4 | Lhotse | 27,923 |
| 5 | Makalu I | 27,824 |
| 6 | Lhotse Shar II | 27,504 |

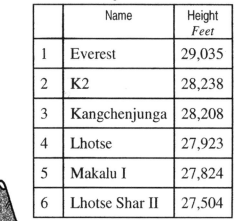

I thought I was the tallest!

Mt. Molehill

**1.** Fill in the missing symbol: <, >, or =.

$$\frac{11}{15} \quad \boxed{\phantom{x}} \quad \frac{8}{9}$$

**2.** Compute: Find the sum of forty-three thousandths and eighty-nine hundredths. Write the answer in standard notation.

**3.** Simplify the expression.

$$\frac{25b}{125} + 3b^2$$

**4.** Find the area of this figure.

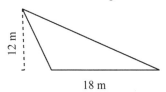

12 m

18 m

Get out your yardsticks.

**5.** The highest living mammal lives in the mountains of Asia at 20,100 feet. The highest altitude marathon took place at 17,100 feet on Mt. Everest. Find the difference between the two altitudes. Write the measurement in inches.

**1.** Compute: **800 x (−36) =**

**2.** A box holds pairs of gloves hooked together: 12 black pairs, eight white, 13 red, and two green. A climber grabs a pair. What is the probability that this pair is neither red nor white?

*Do you need a hand with this problem?*

**3.** Josh climbed 800 feet on Monday, 750 on Tuesday, 850 on Wednesday, 800 on Thursday, and 900 on Friday. Follow the pattern to find how many feet he climbed on Saturday.

**4.** Erin thinks that only two lines of symmetry can be drawn through this figure. Is she right?

**5.** Hiking is one of the fastest-growing recreational activities in the U.S. In 2001, 30,500,000 people participated in the activity. This was a 17% increase over the number in 2000.

Will this equation find the number that participated in 2000?

**x + 0.17x = 30,500,000**

**1.** The fastest climb of Mt. Everest took just under 11 hours. The fastest climb of the same altitude on a climbing machine took just under 3 hours. Write a ratio to compare the machine climb to the real climb.

**2.** Compute: $\frac{1}{10} \div \frac{7}{8} =$

**3.** Which object would weigh about 15 kg?

○ **an eraser**      ○ **a school bus**

○ **a full backpack**      ○ **a large bear**

○ **a basketball**      ○ **a cupcake**

**4.** If n is 6, what is p?
**p = −2n**

**5.** Tamae Watanabe of Japan is the oldest woman to reach the summit of Mt. Everest. She accomplished this on May 16, 2002. At the time she was 63 years, 177 days old. When was she born?

*Now, that's a time to beat!*

*Name*

**1.** Estimate the quotient.

**28,945 ÷ 625 =**

Easy!

**3.** Compute: **2(16,000 − 3500 + 1200) =**

**2.** The total measurement of a pair of two complementary angles and two straight angles is

○ 360°          ○ 720°

○ 540°          ○ 180°

**4.** Four friends climbed a mountain: Maria, Evan, Henry, and Kayla. They all reached the summit on the same day. How many different combinations are possible for the order in which they reached the summit?

## 5. Challenge Problem

The diagram shows the path some climbers followed to climb and descend the mountain. Use the Pythagorean theorem ($a^2 + b^2 = c^2$) to find the distance of their descent.

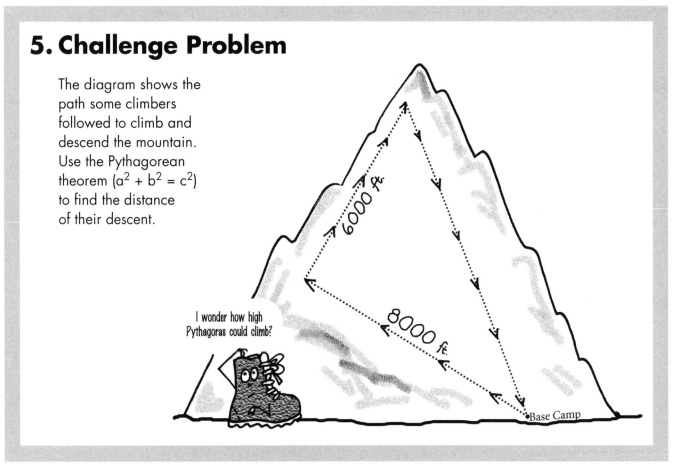

I wonder how high Pythagoras could climb?

**1.** Compute: 65 ‾‾‾‾‾‾‾195,000

I'm just a chip off
the old potato.

**2.** In 1637, William Harvey discovered how blood circulates through the body. This was 292 years before Alexander Fleming discovered penicillin. What year was this second discovery made?

**3.** Each prime number between 0 and 20 is written on a piece of paper and put into a box. One paper is drawn. How many different outcomes are possible?

**4.** Draw a flip of this figure.

**5.** Which equation will solve the problem?

**Potato chips were invented in 1853. Just 150 years later, Americans were using 192.5 billion pounds of potatoes a year to make potato chips. If people under 25 eat 55 percent of the chips produced, how many pounds of potatoes are they eating in the form of chips?**

___ a. $0.55p = 192,500,000,000$

___ b. $p = 192,500,000,000 \times 0.55$

___ c. $192,500,000,000 \times 55 = p$

**1.** A high school student named C.J. invented 144 new ice cream flavors in 864 days. At this rate, how many flavors did he invent in 216 days?

How about Eggplant Swirl?
Or, Onion-Marmalade?

**2.** Compute: **152.81 ÷ 3.02 =**

**3.** Solve the equation.

**134 = 7c − 10 + 5c**

**4.** Write four fractions that are equivalent to $\frac{18}{30}$.

**5.** The sundial was one of the earliest human inventions.

The volume of this sundial is
   a. 17,584 cm$^3$
   b. 4396 cm$^3$
   c. 125.6 cm$^3$
   d. 25,120 cm$^3$
   e. 439.6 cm$^3$
   f. 140 cm$^3$

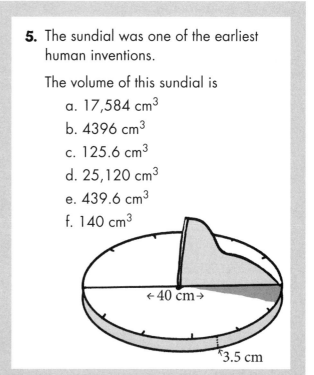

← 40 cm →

3.5 cm

**1.** Find d if c = –11.

$$-d + 4c = -104$$

**2.** The Wright Brothers' flying machine, *The Flyer,* was 6.4 m long. The modern Boeing 747 airplane is 11.09 times this long. How long is the 747 (rounded to the nearest meter)?

*You could say I've got the Wright stuff.*

**3.** Fill in the missing number.

$$-98 - 42 + \boxed{\phantom{00}} = -149$$

**4.** How many diagonals can be drawn in a decagon?

**5.** Between which inventions did more years pass?

___ a. printing press & safety pin

___ b. jet engine & cash register

___ c. thermometer & zipper

| Invention | Year |
|-----------|------|
| printing press | 1454 |
| thermometer | 1592 |
| jet engine | 1930 |
| zipper | 1892 |
| submarine | 1898 |
| neon lights | 1910 |
| cash register | 1879 |
| safety pin | 1849 |

**1.** Compute: $13\frac{2}{9} + 133\frac{1}{3} =$

**2.** Which tool is best for measuring the size of an angle?

○ meter stick      ○ protractor

○ scale            ○ thermometer

**3.** Use words to write this number: 0.0616

**4.** Which number pairs will solve the equation:

$$2x - y = 4?$$

(5,6);  (–3, –10);  (12, –8)  (0, –4)

*Mental math...again?*

**5.** Use mental math to arrive at an estimated solution to the problem.

From 1977 to 2001, the number of patents registered in the U. S. was 4,380,088. Among the most frequent kinds of patented new products were prescription or over-the-counter drugs. There were a total of 114,996 new drug patents. How many patents were for something other than drugs?

**1.** Which property is shown here?

463.9 x 1 = 463.9

0 x 87.065 = 0

$\frac{1}{4} + 0 = \frac{1}{4}$

8000 x 1 = 8000

225 x 0 = 0

$97^2$ x 0 = 0

**2.** Simplify the equation

**10t + t – 135 = 365 + t**

**3.** Is this computation correct?

**365 x 999 = 354,635**

**4.** A permutation is

___ a. the projection of future possible outcomes

___ b. an arrangement of data in a definite order

___ c. the numerical likelihood of one chosen outcome in comparison to another outcome

___ d. an event whose outcome affects future events

___ e. the selection of a set of things from a larger set

## 5. Challenge Problem

A. How many triangles are in this figure?

_____

B. How many parallelograms are in this figure?

_____

C. How many trapezoids are in this figure?

_____

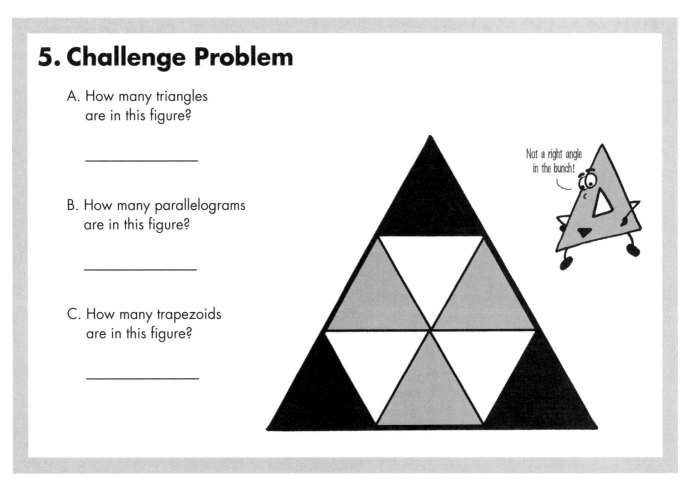

Not a right angle in the bunch!

1. Which would be the best way to show a comparison of the amounts of wedding cake eaten at ten large weddings?

   ○ a scattergram          ○ a circle graph

   ○ a bar graph            ○ a double line graph

   ○ a tally sheet          ○ a diagram

2. Simplify the equation.

   $$\frac{12n}{6} + 20 = 4n$$

3. Several record-breaking pizzas have these weights: 7 pounds, 9 pounds, 6 pounds, 8 pounds, 5 pounds, 9 pounds, and 12 pounds.

   Compute the average of these weights.

4. Draw an irregular hexagon.
   (All the sides will not be the same length.)

5. The largest wedding cake ever made weighed about 1500 pounds. Assume that:

   tier one had $\frac{1}{20}$ the total weight

   tier two had $\frac{1}{15}$ the total weight

   tier three had $\frac{2}{15}$ the total weight

   tier four had $\frac{1}{6}$ the total weight

   tier five had $\frac{1}{3}$ the total weight.

   What was the weight of the fifth tier?

1. Compute: **10.011 x 0.101 =**

2. The largest serving of fish and chips (fries) ever recorded weighed 72 pounds. The fish weighed 31 pounds. What percent of the total weight was made up by the chips?

3. Round to the nearest ten thousandth.

   **100.032487**

4. Find the rule of this input-output table. Fill in the missing numbers.

| Input | Output |
|-------|--------|
| 20    | 11     |
| 16    | 9      |
| 15    | 8.5    |
| 12    | 7      |
| 10    |        |
|       | 5      |
| 4     |        |

5. This is a scale drawing of the world's largest pumpkin pie.

   A. Find the pie's diameter.

   B. Find the pie's circumference.
      *(Round to the nearest tenth.)*

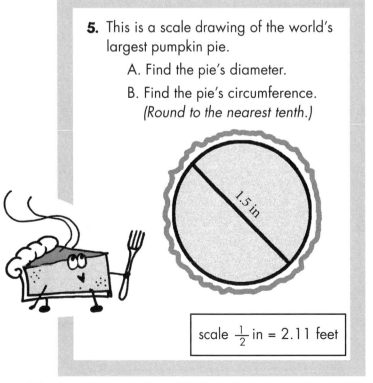

1.5 in

scale $\frac{1}{2}$ in = 2.11 feet

**1.** The largest box of popcorn in the world held a volume of 880 ft$^3$ of popcorn. It took about six hours to fill the box. Find the rate per minute.
*(Round to the nearest tenth.)*

**2.** Compute: **−85 − (−12) =**

**3.** Louie has four books about unusual facts on his bookshelf. How many different permutations (arrangements) are possible for these books?

**4.** Solve the equation.

$$20 = m + \frac{4}{9}$$

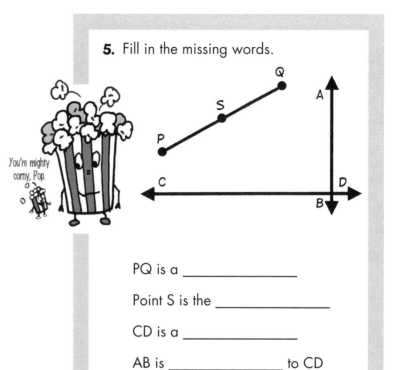

**5.** Fill in the missing words.

PQ is a _____

Point S is the _____

CD is a _____

AB is _____ to CD

**1.** The world's largest cup of coffee held 394.7 gallons of cappuccino. The largest milkshake was 22,712 liters. Which drink was larger?

**2.** Write each fraction in lowest terms.

a. $\frac{9}{12}$    b. $\frac{22}{88}$

c. $\frac{67}{3}$    d. $\frac{18}{30}$

**3.** Compute:    $\frac{6}{9} \times \frac{1}{3} =$

**4.** Draw the graph of $\leq -1$.

**5.** Solve the problem. Tell how you arrived at the solution.

**The largest bowl of pasta in the world weighed 3,265 pounds. Assume that half of the total weight was eaten by people who ate one quarter pound each, and that the rest was eaten by people who ate one half pound each. What was the total number of pasta-eaters?**

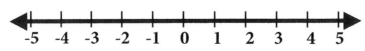

**84**

*Name*

**1.** Fill in the missing operation.

$$\frac{2}{3} \; \boxed{\phantom{x}} \; \frac{3}{5} = \frac{2}{5}$$

**3.** Solve the equation.

$$-30f - 25 = 425$$

**2.** The largest tea bag could make 3,500 cups of tea. It was 10 feet tall and 7.25 feet wide.

Use the formula **A = lw** to compute the area of one flat side of the bag.

What did the tea bag say?

I'm always getting into hot water.

**4.** Define range for a set of statistical data. Give the range of the data on this table.

| TALLEST & LONGEST | |
|---|---|
| bag of cookies | 128 in |
| lollipops | 118 in |
| sesame twist | 58 in |
| salami | 5980 in |
| candy cane | 432 in |
| box of popcorn | 480 in |

# 5. Challenge Problem

I'm a pizza with pizzaz!

The largest pizza that is sold commercially is available from Paul Revere's Pizza Company. The pizza has a 4-foot diameter and costs about $100.00.

a. What is the circumference of the pizza?

b. If the pizza was sliced by cutting eight diameters with a pizza cutter, how may slices would be created?

c. Sliced according to B (above), what is the measurement of the outside edge of each of the slices?

d. Sliced according to B (above) what is the cost per slice?

**1.** Compute:  **123,456 x 78 =**

**2.** A bag contains 24 basketballs: 18 blue and 6 orange. A player reaches in and grabs a ball without looking. What are the **odds against** the ball being orange?

*It's in the bag.*

**3.** Which operation should be done last when solving this equation?

$$x(6 - 14) + 2y(9 \div 3) = 32$$

**4.** Sam shoots a total of 77,500 free throws during games and practices in his basketball career. 27,125 go in the basket. Dave hits 7,300 out of 8,250 free throws in his career. Which player has a better percentage of success?

**5.** Name the line segment that is a tangent.

**1.** A basketball player's salary is $1,597,500 a year. He makes 3,550 points in one season. Calculate the amount he earns per point.

**2.** Write this number in scientific notation.

**98,300,000,000**

*I'm having a ball.*

**3.** Use words to write this equation.

$$n\left(\frac{210}{7}\right) = 600$$

**4.** Reggie Miller set a record for the most three-point field goals in the NBA with 2,526 of them. Karl Malone made 9,715 free throws to set the record for this feat. Find the difference in points between these two accomplishments.

**5.** Use a ruler and the scale below to find the height of this basket.

Scale $\frac{1}{2}$ in = $1\frac{1}{2}$ ft

1. How many vertices are on a prism with a pentagonal base?

| | | |
|---|---|---|
| **10** | **5** | **7** |
| **15** | **20** | **12** |

2. Compute:

   **–12 x (–37) x (–18) =**

3. What number has a value opposite to 9,000?

It's a slam dunk.

4. As of the end of the 2003 NBA season, Kareem Abdul-Jabbar held the record as the highest-scoring NBA player (in regular season games). Solve this problem to find the number of points he scored in his career.

   **$-1363 + 200^2 - \sqrt{62,500} =$**

5. Find the mean of these statistics.

| Season Rebounds | |
|---|---|
| Alexis | 13 |
| Tasha | 16 |
| Janice | 18 |
| Debra | 23 |
| Simone | 16 |
| Lee | 10 |

1. Solve the equation

   **88 = –6y – y + 39**

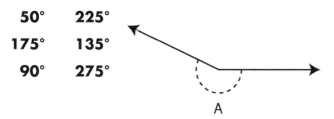

I toe the line.

2. Write this number as a fraction and a decimal:

   **2.16%**

3. Compute:   **$5\frac{1}{2} \div 5\frac{5}{6} =$**

4. The measure of Angle A is closest to

| | |
|---|---|
| **50°** | **225°** |
| **175°** | **135°** |
| **90°** | **275°** |

A

5. Solve the problem. Explain how you solved it.

   **The longest basketball marathon was played in Bermuda in 2003. It lasted 26 hours and 42 minutes. Assuming that it began on a Friday morning at 9:20 am, and that there were breaks making the total time 28 hours, what time did the tournament begin?**

**1.** Compute:

**6200 x 3000 =**

○ 186    ○ 1,860,000

○ 1,860    ○ 18,600

○ 1,800    ○ 18,600,000

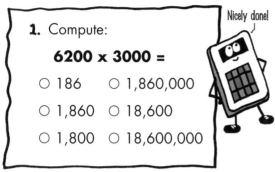

Nicely done!

**2.** Simplify the expression.

**$12 + 8x^9 \div 2x^5 + 36$**

**3.** Compute:
**$855 + 1300 - ( 2500 + 6^3) =$**

**4.** Set up a proportion to solve this problem.

A basketball player earns $9,750 in 15 games. At this rate, how many games will it take him to make $35,750?

## 5. Challenge Problem

Members of a basketball team are painting a design on the floor of the basketball court. The special paint they are buying costs $15.80 a pint. One pint of this paint covers ten square feet of surface.

A. How much blue paint will they need to buy? _____

B. How much red paint will they need to buy? _____

C. How much will the paint cost for the whole job? _____

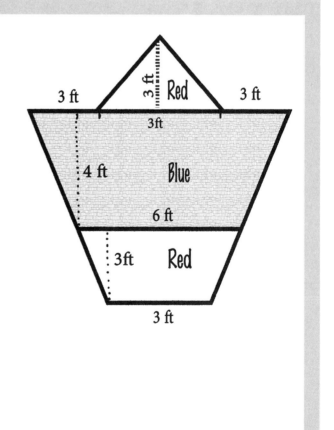

**1.** Find the surface area of this figure.

**2.** The largest game of musical chairs on record started with 8,238 participants. The game ended after $3\frac{1}{2}$ hours with one winner, Xu Chon Wei. How many participants were eliminated per half hour? *(Round to the nearest whole number.)*

**3.** Compute:  **55,050,050**
     **– 505,505**

**4.** What comes next?

**5.** A music store bought and sold copies of old sheet music. Their collection included 12,000 different sheets. The manager looked at 200 sheets and found that "Rudolph The Red-Nosed Reindeer" showed up 67 times. Use this proportion to predict how many times the "Rudolph" song was found in the 12,000 sheets of music.

**1.** Compute: **56 – 3.456 =**

**2.** An old jukebox plays songs at random.

There are 7 jazz tunes, 15 rock tunes, 4 hip hop tunes, and 9 country tunes. Charlie puts in money and a song plays. What is the probability that it will not be a rock tune?

**3.** 40 inches = _____ centimeters

**4.** Shana has $399.70 in dimes. How many dimes does she have?

**5.** The Beatles, Elvis Presley, and the Rolling Stones are the musical artists with the most #1-selling music albums. The sum of their #1 albums is 37. The Beatles had 10 more than either Elvis or the Stones. How many #1 sellers did Elvis have?

Choose the equation that will solve the problem.

___ a. $x + 10 = \frac{37}{2}$

___ b. $2x + (x + 10) = 37$

___ c. $37 - 10 = x$

___ d. $(x - 10) + (x + 10) = 37$

*Name*

**1.** Explain the difference between **similar** and **congruent** figures.

**2.** What operation should be done first?

The first female to sell over 1 million records was American blues singer Bessie Smith. The record cost 75¢ and sold 2 million copies. Two-fifths of these sold in the first year. How much money did the record make in that year?

**3.** Solve the equation.

$3(4 + 12b) - b = 82$

Some hits are on the flip side.

**4.** Compute:
$-7,000 + 35 + (-16) =$

**5.** Draw a flip of the figure in the right-hand quadrant of the grid.

*Name*

**1.** Write the smallest whole number that can be written with these digits: 3, 0, 1, 9, 8, 3, 0.

**2.** Simplify the equation.

$12p + \frac{18}{6} - 4p = -17$

**3.** Compute: $\frac{8}{15} + \frac{7}{12} =$

**4.** A 2003 Bruce Springsteen concert series attended by a total of 566,560 fans took in $38,684,050. Which is closest to the average ticket price?

| | | |
|---|---|---|
| $70 | $100 | $35 |
| $140 | $50 | $20 |

**5.** Which note has the second largest area? *(Do not consider the stem of the note.)*

A

2 cm

B

4.5 cm

2 cm

C

2 cm

5 cm

**1.** Is the computation correct?

$$18 \overline{)6338} \quad 352 \text{ R } 2$$

**2.** Which operation should be done last?

$$20n + \frac{70}{10} + 5^2 =$$

**3.** Find the perimeter of this figure.

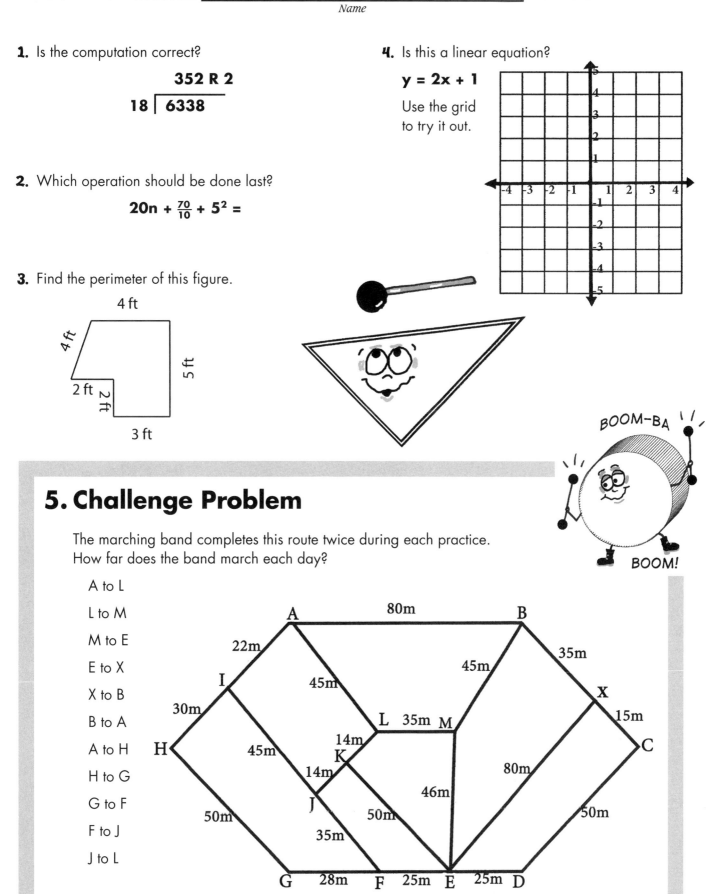

4 ft

4 ft

2 ft  2 ft

5 ft

3 ft

**4.** Is this a linear equation?

$$y = 2x + 1$$

Use the grid to try it out.

## 5. Challenge Problem

The marching band completes this route twice during each practice. How far does the band march each day?

A to L

L to M

M to E

E to X

X to B

B to A

A to H

H to G

G to F

F to J

J to L

BOOM-BA

BOOM!

A          80m          B

22m

I                45m              45m        35m

30m                                          X

H          45m        L  35m  M          15m

14m                                    C

K

14m                          80m

J          46m

50m        50m                    50m

G   28m   F   25m   E   25m   D

35m

*Name*

**1.** Use the inverse operation to check this calculation.

$$6888 \div 56 = 123$$

**2.** In 1999, a severe storm in France knocked over or split 270 million trees. The storm lasted 30 hours. Assuming the rate of 270 million trees to 30 hours, how many trees were felled or split in 12 hours?

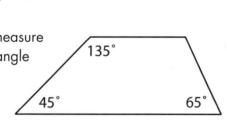

What a sad story.

**3.** Solve the equation.

$$k + 3(k - 4) = k + 27$$

**4.** What is the measure of the fourth angle in this figure?

135°
45°      65°

**5.** Find the mode and median in this set of statistics.

| Frequency of Natural Disasters 1993–2002 | |
| --- | --- |
| *Type* | *# of Events* |
| Droughts | 263 |
| Floods | 1075 |
| Earthquakes | 229 |
| Windstorms | 823 |
| Extreme Temperatures | 138 |
| Avalanches/Landslides | 187 |
| Volcano Eruptions | 52 |
| Forest Fires | 138 |

*Name*

**1.** What are the variables in this expression?

$$7a^3 + 4a - 12b + 25$$

Express yourself.

**2.** The coldest place on Earth, Vostok, Antarctica, measured –138.6°F. The hottest place, Al Aziziyah, Libya, had a temperature of 136.4°F. Write and solve a problem with positive and negative numbers that will find the difference between the two temperatures.

**3.** Compute:  $16.3 \overline{)41.565}$

**4.** Which numbers are divisible by 4?

732      994      442      5,000

8,483      904      776

**5.** Fill in the missing measurements.

A.  12 lb = _____ oz

B.  300 kg = _____ g

C.  _____ sec = 7 hr

D.  66 ft = _____ in

E.  2640 ft = _____ mi

F.  _____ ft² = 12 yd²

G.  68 pt = _____ gal

H.  _____ acres = 87,120 ft²

I.  25 m = _____ mm

J.  96 T = _____ C

K.  _____ cm³ = 4 L

L.  92 kg = _____ g

1. The greatest number of tornados reported in the U.S. in a 24-hour period swept through the midwest and south in 1974. In all, 148 tornados were reported. What was the average number of tornados per hour?

2. Compute:

   $-77 \div 0.77 =$

3. Solve the equation:

   $2(g - 5) + 27.6 = 0$

Oops!

4. A figure has four faces, six edges, and one vertex. What is the figure? What is the shape of its base?

5. Finish the tree diagram to show the outcome of one spin for each of two different spinners. One spinner has three equal sections: red, green, blue. The other has four equal sections labeled: 1, 2, 3, 4.

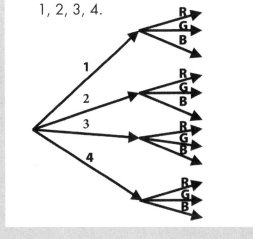

1. Compute: $\frac{1}{2} \times \frac{1}{3} \times \frac{1}{5} =$

2. Jed tracked a storm for five days. The wind speeds were: Mon–175.6 mph; Tue–155.5 mph; Wed–125.4 mph; Thur–85.3 mph. What is the wind speed likely to be on Friday?

I come from Pencil-vania.

3. Simplify the expression.

   $10(c^2 + c - 4) + 7c^3 + 9$

4. On Saturday, October 1, Joey started counting to a million, counting one number every second without stopping. Provided he stayed awake, on what day did he reach 1 million?

5. The longest lightning flash ever measured had a surprising horizontal distance. Measure this diagram to find out how much distance it spanned. *(Round to the nearest whole number.)*

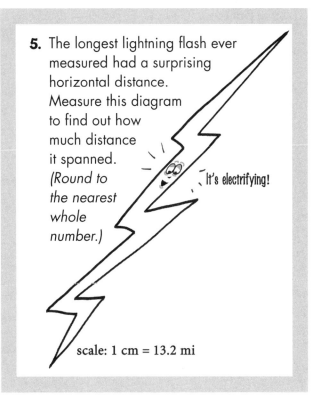

It's electrifying!

scale: 1 cm = 13.2 mi

**1.** Is the computation correct?

$$\begin{array}{r} \$80,800.00 \\ -\ \ \ 8,088.00 \\ \hline \$72,822.00 \end{array}$$

**3.** Estimate the answer:

**689 x 32 x 512 =**

**2.** The driest place on Earth is in the Atacama Desert, Chile. From 1964 to 2001, only 18.5 mm of rainfall were measured in this location. Lee estimated that the desert received 0.005 mm per year for each of those years. Is this a reasonable measurement?

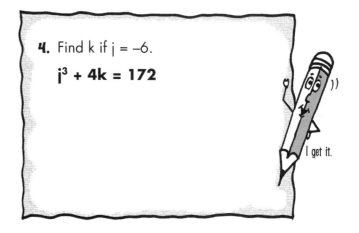

**4.** Find k if j = –6.

$$j^3 + 4k = 172$$

I get it.

## 5. Challenge Problem

Place the numbers 1-9 in the squares so that each column, each row, and each diagonal give a sum of 15. Use each of the numbers only once.

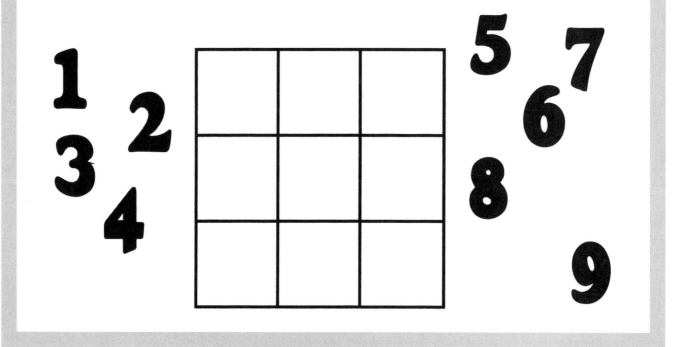

**1.** What information is missing that is needed to solve this problem?

The comic strip syndicated most is Garfield. It is published in 2,570 different newspapers or journals and read by 263 million readers in 11 countries. What percentage of the Garfield readers are in North America?

**2.** Compute:  **222 | 19,544**

**3.** In a stack of 100 newspapers, the comic section is missing from 60 papers. Lexie buys two papers from the stack. What is the probability that both papers will have the comic section?

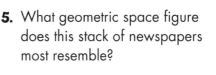

EXTRA! EXTRA!
Math in the news!

**4.** Find two number pairs that will solve the equation:

**5x = 3y**

**5.** What geometric space figure does this stack of newspapers most resemble?

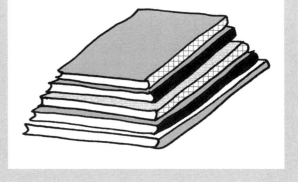

**1.** Arianna delivers newspapers six mornings a week. Her route is 5.7 k long. How many meters does she travel in one week?

I have newsprint in my blood.

**2.** Compute:

**8,003 x – 0.15 =**

**3.** What is the LCM of **7** and **12**?

**4.** Is this a correct graph of **x > –20?**

-50  -40  -30  -20  -10  0  10  20  30  40  50

**5.** A city newspaper needs nine tons of papers delivered each weekday. A delivery person can carry 35 pounds in a backpack and another 25 pounds in the bicycle basket. Each carrier makes two trips a day, refilling the backpack and the basket after the first trip. How many delivery persons should the newspaper company hire?

*Name*

**1.** Compute:     **–96 – 17 – (–3) =**

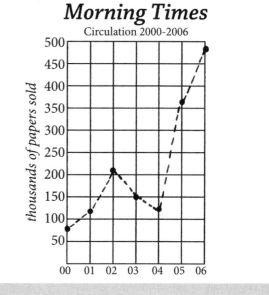

Does that include leap year?

**2.** The first comic strip published was *The Yellow Kid*. It appeared on October 18, 1896. How many days have passed since then?

**3.** Simplify the expression.

$$8y^2(4y^6 + 2)$$

**4.** Draw an ***isosceles triangle***.

**5.** From this data, make a generalization about the change in the paper's circulation from 2000 to 2006.

### Morning Times
Circulation 2000-2006

*thousands of papers sold*

00 01 02 03 04 05 06

---

*Name*

**1.** What is nine divided by seven-eighths?

**2.** Which operation should be done first?

**1,094,000 people read the *New York Times* Monday – Saturday, and the paper is read by 1,650,000 on Sunday. Compute the average number of *Times* papers read each day.**

**3.** True or false: *A repeating decimal is an irrational number.*

**4.** Solve the equation.

$$164 = 6a^2 - 4(a^2 + 9)$$

I read it in the *Times*.

**5.** Newspaper readers use this recycling bin in the subway to dispose of their newspapers. What is the container's volume?

80 cm

150 cm

MUNCH

**1.** Fill in the missing operation.

$$8{,}553 \boxed{\phantom{+}} 6{,}989 = 1{,}564$$

**2.** I am a two-digit prime number. The product of my digits is less than five and the sum of my digits is divisible by four. Who am I?

**3.** A company paid these prices for the same advertisement placed in six different magazines:

| | | |
|---|---|---|
| $629,000 | $30,000 | $355,000 |
| $5,200 | $198,000 | $830 |

What is the average cost of this ad?

**4.** One edition of the New York Times had 1,612 pages. This is 20 fewer than 48 times the number of pages in a paper put out by students at Logan Middle School. How many pages were in the middle school paper?

Which equation is best to find the solution for this problem?

a. 48(20 + n) = 1612

b. 48n – 20 = 1612

c. 1612 = 48n + 20

d. n(48–20) = 1612

Use your head.

# 5. Challenge Problem

A commuter stops at a newspaper stand in northern California and finds a pile of each of the following papers for sale:

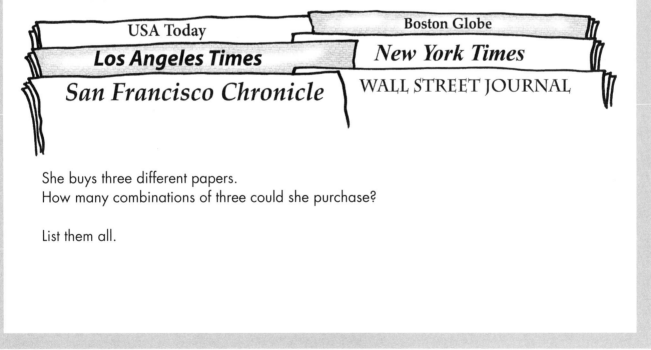

USA Today
Los Angeles Times
San Francisco Chronicle
Boston Globe
New York Times
WALL STREET JOURNAL

She buys three different papers.
How many combinations of three could she purchase?

List them all.

**1.** Compute:    **6,000 x 444 =**

**2.** Charlene climbed 6,234 feet in elevation bouncing on a pogo stick. Terry climbed two-thirds that height. Max climbed three-fourths the height that Terry climbed. How many feet did Max climb?

**3.** Is the number pair (3, –9) (x = 3 and y = –9) a solution to the equation below?

$$13x^2 + 3y = 99 + y$$

**4.** Name this figure.

How many faces? _____

How many edges? _____

How many vertices? _____

**5.** How many records were set with a distance more than ten times the distance of the cricket spit?

## Strange Tosses

| Sport | Record Distance |
|---|---|
| rolling pin toss | 53.47 m |
| plastic disc toss | 250 m |
| card throw | 65.96 m |
| cricket spit | 6.82 m |
| cow pie throw | 81.1 m |
| boot toss | 63.98 m |

**1.** Compute: **80.05 – 20.557 =**

**2.** To win the longest ironing marathon, Eufemia Stadler ironed for 40 hours. If she started October 16 at 9:55 a.m., and took a total of 36 hr, 40 min to sleep, when did she finish?

**3.** Simplify the expression.

$$121 + 5x + 4y^2 - 3x + 14$$

**4.** Round these to the nearest whole number

$7\frac{5}{7}$     $\frac{8}{11}$     $16\frac{2}{3}$     $\frac{19}{4}$     $30\frac{6}{12}$

**5.** A rolling pin-throwing champion bragged that the average of his six best tosses is 50 ft, 11 inches. The distances of the six tosses are listed below. Is the champion's claim reasonable?

     1. 40 ft, 7 in

     2. 48 ft, 6 in

     3. 51 ft, 10 in

     4. 36 ft, 6 in

     5. 42 ft, 3 in

     6. 39 ft, 8 in

**1.** True or false?

___ a. All perpendicular lines
are intersecting lines.

___ b. Parallel lines never intersect.

Well, color me orange.

**2.** Use words to write
this expression.

$30n + \frac{1}{2}m$

**3.** An umbrella stand has one umbrella
in each of these colors: red, purple,
black, green, yellow, and white.
A man takes one umbrella without looking. Then he
flips a coin. How many outcomes are possible for
these two events? List them.

**4.** Compute:     $-330 \times 5(x - 13) =$

**5.** What operation should be done first
when solving this problem?

Ashrita Furman, who
holds 19 Guinness World
Records, walked 80.96
miles in about 24 hours
carrying a bottle of milk
on his head. He also
bounced about 23 miles
on a pogo stick in 12.5
hours. What is the
difference in rate per
hour in these two feats?

**1.** Compute:

$\frac{2}{17} + \frac{12}{34} =$

Card-flipping
makes me
loopy.

**2.** What is the coefficient of $b^2$?

$3b + 4b^2 - 5b + b^3$

**3.** Round to the nearest hundred.

**835,279,067**

**4.** Which figure has the greater surface area?

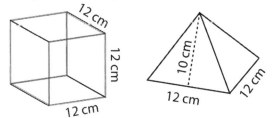

**5.** Lucy practiced throwing cards for
four hours for an upcoming card-
throwing competition. The chart
gives some information about the
number she threw each hour.
Write an equation to find out
how many she threw in the
second hour.

| | |
|---|---|
| 1st hour | 60 cards |
| 2nd hour | ? |
| 3rd hour | twice the 2nd hour |
| 4th hour | 35 more than 2nd hour |
| Total in 4 hours = 395 cards | |

**1.** Estimate to decide which quotient is greater.

   **a.** $22\overline{)8395}$

   **b.** 13,888 ÷ 47 =

**2.** Compute:

   **7,000,000 ÷ 35,000 =**

**3.** Solve the equation.

$$3x^2 + 137 = 500$$

Could **x** also be the opposite of the number you found?

**4.** Twelve thousand people signed up for a competition in such strange sports as boot-tossing and cricket-spitting. The program manager examined the first 200 applicants and found that the name Smith was the last name of 38 of them. Using this information, how many people of the 12,000 do you predict will have the name Smith?

## 5. Challenge Problem

Use mental math to solve the problem.

**Two brothers practice together to improve their boot-throwing skills. They each have a good chance of setting new records in their age categories. The product of the ages of two boot-tossers is 108. The sum of their ages is greater than 20 and less than 40. Find all the possible ages for this pair.**

They gave me the boot!

**1.** Compute: **80,000 x 500 =**

**2.** In 2002, $5.54 \times 10^7$ people in the U.S. participated in overnight camping as a recreational activity. By 2003, this number had increased to 11,080,000. How many campers were there in 2003? (Write the answer in scientific notation.)

**3.** Will the answer be a positive or negative number?

$$-b^3 + (-12) =$$

**4.** Name this figure.

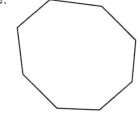

**5.** Will brought a whole bag of snacks along on his camping trip. The bag had:

5 chocolate bars

6 granola bars

4 peanut butter bars

3 toffee bars

All the bars were of equal size and shape. Will took two bars from the bag. What is the probability that they were both granola bars?

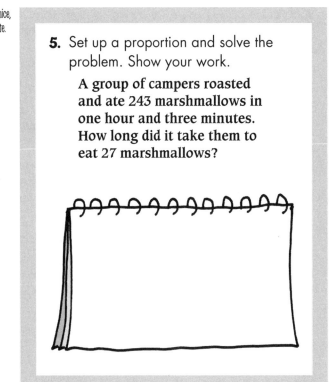

**1.** Simplify the equation.

**724 + x = 12(3x + 2)**

*Marshmallows are nice, but I prefer graphite.*

**2.** Write the fractions in lowest terms.

$$\frac{12}{180} \qquad \frac{37}{3} \qquad \frac{59}{118}$$

**3.** Scott's backpack weighed 551 oz. Tyler's backpack weighed 7 lb, 12 oz less. What was the weight of Tyler's pack (in pounds and ounces)?

**4.** Compute: **10.1 ÷ 0.101 =**

**5.** Set up a proportion and solve the problem. Show your work.

**A group of campers roasted and ate 243 marshmallows in one hour and three minutes. How long did it take them to eat 27 marshmallows?**

**1.** Give the measure of each angle.

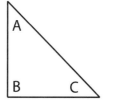

**2.** Compute:

**−18 − 6 − (−3) =**

**3.** Solve the equation.

**−n = 12n − 165**

**4.** Dion's new tent is 8 percent of the total weight of his full backpack. The pack weighs 42.75 lb. What is the weight of the sleeping bag?

Everybody's got an angle!

**5.** Plot these points and connect them in order:

A. (−4, 1)  D. (2, 7)  G. (−4, 1)
B. (−2, 7)  E. (4, 1)  H. (−2, 4)
C. (0, 6.5)  F. (0, 1)  I. (0, 1)

**1.** Compute:  $\frac{1}{30} \times \frac{30}{1} \times \frac{1}{10} =$

I'm ready for some change.

**2.** Find 12 different ways to change a $50 bill.

**3.** Solve the problem. Write the answer in scientific notation.

$$(7.76 \times 10^8)(2.0 \times 10^5) =$$

**4.** Write a number that is 12.005 less than 69.7405.

**5.** What measurement unit would you use to find . . .

    a. the capacity of a tent?
    b. the height of a backpack?
    c. the diameter of a blister?
    d. the temperature of a stream?
    e. the weight of a hiker?
    f. the length of a sleeping bag?
    g. the weight of a mosquito?

**1.** Which is greater?

    a. 25% of $1360.00

    b. 15% of $2110.00

**3.** The value of $8.163 \times 10^6$ is

    a. 81,630,000

    b. 8,163,000

    c. 8,016,300,000

    d. 816,300,000

**2.** Is this solution accurate?

$$k + 30k - k^2 = 220$$
$$k = 30$$

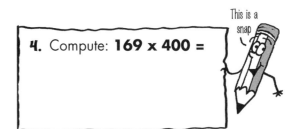

This is a snap

**4.** Compute: **169 x 400 =**

# 5. Challenge Problem

By the time the five campers get to their campsite, each one has an ailment: poison ivy, a fever, blisters, a sprained ankle, or sunburn. Each is in a separate tent. Use the clues and the diagram to figure out who has the sprained ankle.

**Clues:**

• The person with a fever is tenting between the person with poison ivy and the person with blisters.

• Anya's tent is between Laura's and Henry's.

• Grant and Henry have tents on the ends.

• The person with the fever is next to Grant.

• A person on the end has sunburn.

• Laura is in Tent #3.

• Laura does not have poison ivy.

• The camper in Tent #2 has a fever.

• Teryl wore plenty of sunscreen.

• A boy has a fever.

• Teryl is next to Laura.

*Name*

**1.** Compute:

```
   19,159
   86,301
 + 12,819
```

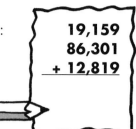

**2.** There are 14 socks in a drawer: 6 black and 8 white. A girl chooses two. What is the probability of 2 whites?

**3.** Simplify the expression.

$$\frac{45}{x} = 1395$$

**4.** How many faces are found on a rectangular pyramid?

Oh, buoy!

**5.** Poom Lim of the UK Merchant Navy survived longer alone on a raft at sea than anyone else on record. The ordeal began when his ship was torpedoed on November 23, 1942. He was rescued on April 15, 1943. How many days was he drifting alone on the sea?

*Name*

**1.** Compute: **90.7 x 9.07 =**

**2.** When an airliner blew up on January 26, 1972, flight attendant Vesna Vulovic survived a fall of 10,160 meters without a parachute. Estimate the number of feet of this fall.

I hope you float.

**3.** Solve the equation.

**30c + 12 + 4(c – 10) = 108**

**4.** A ship has 324 people and 27 life rafts. Write a ratio showing the relationship of rafts to people.

**5.** Find the surface area of the figure.

4 m

5 m

**1.** The lowest body temperature recorded was 57.5° F. This was measured in a child who was mistakenly locked outside for several hours on a –8° F night. What is the difference between the outdoor temperature and the body temperature?

**2.** Toss a pair of dice. What is the probability of a two-digit result?

**3.** 2°  –6°  –26°  5°  41°  11°  –6°

The mode of these temperatures is

   a. 3°       c. 2°       e. 97°
   b. –26°     d. –6°      f. 5°

**4.** Figure A has these sides: 4 in, 4.6in, and 7 in. Figure B has these sides: 4 in, 7 in, 4.6 in, and 9 in. Could these figures be similar?

**5.** Is this a correct graph of the equation:

$$2x - 1 = y?$$

**THURSDAY** WEEK 34 _____ **MATH** PRACTICE
*Name*

**1.** Compute:     $3\frac{1}{3} \div 1\frac{2}{3} =$

Once, I was trapped in a briefcase for 3 months.

**2.** The measure of one angle in a parallelogram is 113°. The measure of another angle is 67°. What are the measures of the other angles?

**3.** In the statement **3 – n ≥ 14**, which of these could be **n**?

**–30**    **0**    **15**    **–11**    **–10**    **–15**

**4.** Is this a correct statement?

$$\frac{3}{5} = \frac{51}{85}$$

**5.** Kively Papajohn of Cyprus is the person who survived the longest time trapped in an elevator. His age at the time had these characteristics:

- 2-digit even number
- product of digits < 50
- difference between digits = 1
- digit in ones place < digit in tens place
- both digits > 5

**1.** Finish the equation to demonstrate the
***distributive property.***

$$\frac{1}{2}(c + 90 + 8) =$$

**3.** Write an equation to match the words.

**Sixty-six less than a number (k)
equals negative forty-four.**

**2.** The deepest underwater escape on record took
place when American Richard Slater escaped
from a submersible at a depth of –225 feet.
A math student calculated that this depth was
–2,710 inches. Is this a correct calculation?

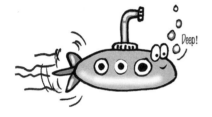

**4.** What is the difference between the area of the
whole figure and the area of the shaded area?

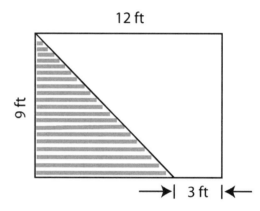

12 ft

9 ft

3 ft

## 5. Challenge Problem

Create a circle graph to show the following data resulting from a survey of 1,000 people who
had survived harrowing events.

### Kinds of Events Survived
#### for 1000 Survivors

| Kind of Event | Number of survivors |
|---|---|
| trapped in elevator | 300 |
| long fall | 150 |
| fall through ice | 380 |
| bear attack | 110 |
| shark attack | 60 |

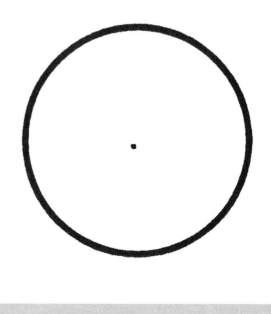

1. The oldest professional baseball player, Leroy Paige, was 708 months and 80 days old. The youngest, Joseph Nuxhall, was 180 months, 314 days old. What is the difference in their ages (in years and days)?

2. Compute:

$$68 \overline{)5236}$$

3. Someone picks a number between 1 and 30. What is the probability that it will be an even number with two digits?

4. Describe the pattern. Tell what is missing.

800  710  630  560  ☐  450  410

5. Finish the drawing to make it symmetrical.

Welcome to first base.

1. Subtract ninety and eleven thousandths from one hundred and one hundredth. Write the answer in standard notation.

2. How many like terms are in this equation?

$$7s + (4s^2 - w) + 3s = w^3 + s$$

3. The Chicago White Sox won the baseball World Series in 2005 after 88 years without a World Series win. In what year was their previous win of the series?

4. A baseball has a 1.43-inch radius. What is its volume?

5. Find the difference between the value of the least and the greatest of these numbers.

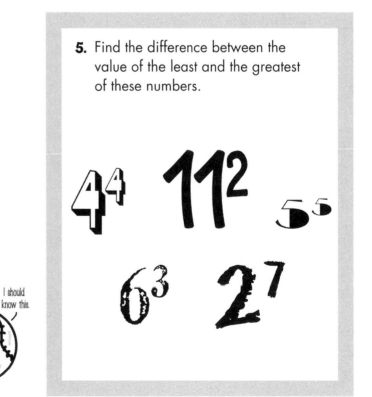

$4^4$  $11^2$  $5^5$  $6^3$  $2^7$

**1.** Compute: **66,300 – (–1,290) =**

**2.** A baseball player kept data on the distance of 150 hits using bats of 20 different lengths. What would be the best way to present the data to show how many hits were made with each length bat?

    ○ bar graph    ○ tally sheet    ○ scattergram

    ○ line graph    ○ pictograph    ○ circle graph

**5.** Estimate the solution to this problem.

**Baseball player Ricky Henderson holds the record for the most stolen bases in a major league career. He stole 1,406 in a career that lasted 24 years. At this rate, how many years did it take to steal 350 bases?**

**3.** Solve the equation.

    **–d – 16 = 2d + (–31)**

**4.** Draw 2 congruent figures.

**1.** Compute: **100 + $\frac{3}{4}$ – $\frac{8}{12}$ =**

Play, ball!

**2.** Since 1903, the New York Yankees have won 26 World Series in 38 appearances in the series. What percentage of the series they played have they lost? (Round to the nearest tenth of a percent.)

**3.** What is the place value of the 7s in this number?

    **970,135.273**

**4.** Which operation should be done first?

    **3n = $\frac{12}{n}$**

**5.** Could the total of the measures of all the angles in this figure be 360°?

**1.** The largest bat was 120 feet long. Find the average length of these replica bats.

| 26 ft | 57 ft | 18 ft |
|-------|-------|-------|
| 14 ft | 43 ft | 76 ft |

Record-breakers have yet to be tied.

**2.** Which is the best estimate for the answer?

$$(19.5 \times \tfrac{1}{2} \times 609) \div 32 =$$

  a. 20          d. 80
  b. 200         e. 800
  c. 2000        f. 8000

**3.** Henry (Hank) Aaron holds the record for the most runs in a major league baseball career. His career lasted from 1954 to 1976. What information do you need to know to determine the average number of runs he scored per year?

**4.** Is this equation simplified correctly?

Equation: $x(2x^3 + 6) = 8x^2 + 1$

Simplified: $2x^4 - 8x^2 + 6x = 12$

## 5. Challenge Problem

Put these fractions in order from least to greatest.

$$\frac{4}{7} \qquad \frac{9}{11} \qquad \frac{9}{13}$$

$$\frac{3}{8} \qquad \frac{4}{5} \qquad \frac{7}{10}$$

*Write fractions here.*

**1.** Compute:
$$\begin{array}{r} 9{,}999 \\ \times\ \ 99 \\ \hline \end{array}$$

**2.** London's Heathrow Airport is the world's busiest airport. A total of 53,796,000 passengers went through this airport in 2001. What was the average number of passengers each month?

**3.** Someone draws the name of a month from a box that has each month's name one time. What is the probability that the month will not have 31 days?

**4.** What geometric figure has 3 faces and 2 edges?

**5.** Which pairs of numbers below (x,y) could be solutions to this equation?

$$5x - 12 = y - 10$$

    a. (5, 23)      e. (0, -2)
    b. (2, 8)      f. (1, 3)
    c. (6, 8)      g. (3, -13)
    d. (10,28)      h. (7, 13)

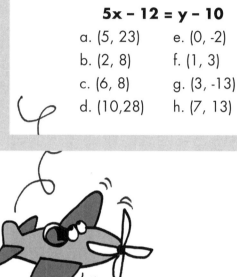

*Sometimes, numbers make me dizzy.*

---

**1.** Compute: **7.5 ÷ 0.003 =**

**2.** Write a proportion that could be used to solve this problem.

**In a skyscraper, 9,450 light bulbs burned out in 15 weeks. At this rate, how many weeks did it take for 3,900 to burn out?**

**3.** If p = −20, what is q?

$$2p^2 + q = -900$$

**4.** Find the area of this figure.

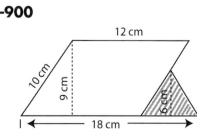

*I see the light.*

**5.** Fill in the missing populations.

**The #1 city has 6,490,728 more people than #5.**

**Houston has 942,385 less than Chicago and 436,081 more than Philadelphia.**

| Top 5 Largest U.S. Cities | |
| --- | --- |
| **City** | **2000 Pop.** |
| New York, NY | |
| Los Angeles, CA | 3,694,820 |
| Chicago, IL | |
| Houston, TX | 1,953,631 |
| Philadelphia, PA | |

**1.** Compute: **(–90 x –30) – (400 x 60) =**

**2.** Nine envelopes each hold a $50 bill.
Five envelopes each hold $100 bills.
The envelopes are put into a box. Someone
draws one envelope. What are the odds in
favor of getting a $100 bill?

  a. $\frac{5}{9}$    c. $\frac{5}{14}$    e. $\frac{9}{5}$

  b. $\frac{9}{14}$    d. $\frac{14}{5}$    f. $\frac{14}{9}$

*Choose me!*

**3.** Simplify the expression.

**88b – 4a + 9(b + a) – 22b**

**4.** Name all angles that are
adjacent to angle EBF.

**5.** What information in the problem is
not necessary for finding the solution?

Tokyo, Japan is the city with the
second most visited theme park in
the world. In 2003, Tokyo's
population was 33.75 million. Also
in 2003, Tokyo Disneyland had
13,188,000 visitors. On the average,
how many people visited Tokyo
Disneyland each month?

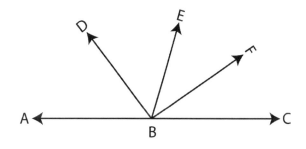

**1.** What percent of 7,300 is 146?

**2.** Compute: $4\frac{1}{8} \times 2\frac{1}{6} =$

**3.** What is the coefficient of $y^2$?

**19 w – y(4 + w) – 3y² + 8y³**

*Give math a
green light.*

**4.** A traffic jam that stretched 109 miles
between Lyon and Paris, France, is the
longest on record. If the average vehicle
was seven feet long, about how many
vehicles were a part of the jam?

**5.** Convert these measurements.

  A.    44 mm = _____ m

  B.  1,300 mL = _____ L

  C.    5 dkm = _____ cm

  D.  9,000 cm = _____ m

  E.    2 km = _____ cm

  F.    330 g = _____ kg

  G.    1 m² = _____ dm²

  H.    30 L = _____ mL

*Name*

**1.** Fill in the missing operations.

$$22 \boxed{\phantom{x}} 55 \boxed{\phantom{x}} 210 = 1,000$$

**2.** Las Vegas, Nevada, has more wedding ceremonies than any other U.S. city. There are 280 ceremonies per day. Assuming ceremonies are performed 24 hours a day, about how long does an average ceremony take?

**3.** Compute:     $90,000 \div 150 =$

○ **6,000**     ○ **60,000**     ○ **4,000**

○ **40**     ○ **4,500**     ○ **600**

**4.** Is the solution accurate?

$$s - s^2 + 50 = 25s - 30$$
$$s = 20$$

This is a list of my peers.

## 5. Challenge Problem

A. Which building has taller stories: Petronas Towers, the Empire State Building, or the International Finance Center?

B. Which building has 19 stories fewer than a building built in 1931?

C. Which building was built more than three decades after the Sears Tower?

D. Which building is 172 feet taller than the Ryogyong Hotel?

E. Which building has 15 fewer stories than the John Hancock Center?

# World's Tallest Buildings

|   | City | Location | Yr Built | Height (ft) | Stories |
|---|------|----------|----------|-------------|---------|
| 1 | Petronas Towers | Kuala Lumpur, Malaysia | 1998 | 1483 | 88 |
| 2 | Taipei 101 | Taipei, Taiwan | 2004 | 1470 + *spire* | 101 |
| 3 | Sears Tower | Chicago, USA | 1974 | 1450 + *spire* | 108 |
| 4 | International Finance Center | Hong Kong, China | 2003 | 1335 + *spire* | 90 |
| 5 | Jin Mao Building | Shanghai, China | 1998 | 1255 + *spire* | 88 |
| 6 | Empire State Building | New York City, USA | 1931 | 1250 + *spire* | 102 |
| 7 | Tuntex 85 Sky Tower | Kao-hsiung, Taiwan | 1997 | 1140 + *spire* | 85 |
| 8 | Aon Center | Chicago, USA | 1973 | 1136 | 83 |
| 9 | John Hancock Center | Chicago, USA | 1968 | 1127 + *spire* | 100 |
| 10 | China World Trade Center | Beijing, China | 2005 | 1083 | 80 |
| 10 | Ryogyong Hotel | Pyongyang, N. Korea | 1992 | 1083 | 105 |

# INCENTIVE PUBLICATIONS DAILY PRACTICE SERIES
## GRADE 8 MATH SKILLS

## Number Concepts

| Skill | 1 | 2 | 3 | 4 | 5 | 6 | 7 | 8 | 9 | 10 | 11 | 12 | 13 | 14 | 15 | 16 | 17 | 18 | 19 | 20 | 21 | 22 | 23 | 24 | 25 | 26 | 27 | 28 | 29 | 30 | 31 | 32 | 33 | 34 | 35 | 36 |
|---|---|---|---|---|---|---|---|---|---|---|---|---|---|---|---|---|---|---|---|---|---|---|---|---|---|---|---|---|---|---|---|---|---|---|---|---|
| Numbers & Systems | √ | | √ | | | √ | | | | | | | √ | √ | √ | √ | √ | | √ | | | | | | | | | | | √ | √ | | | | | |
| Whole numbers: read, write, compare, order | | | | √ | √ | | | | | | | | | √ | | | | | | √ | √ | | | | | | | | | √ | | | | | | |
| Whole numbers: place value | | √ | | | | | | | | | | | √ | | | | √ | | | | | | | √ | | | | | √ | | | | √ | | √ | |
| Whole numbers: rounding | | √ | | | | | | | | | | | | √ | | | | | | √ | | | | | | | | | | | √ | | | | | |
| Multiples, CM, LCM | | | √ | | | | | | | | | √ | | | | | | | | | | | | | | | | | | | √ | | | | | |
| Factors, CF, GCF | | | √ | √ | | | | | √ | | | | | | | | | | | | | | | √ | | | | | | | | | | | | |
| Divisibility | | | | √ | | | | | | | | | | | √ | | | | | | | | | | | | | | | √ | | | | | | |
| Exponential numbers; scientific notation | | √ | √ | √ | | √ | | √ | | | √ | | | | √ | √ | √ | | √ | | √ | | √ | | | | | √ | | √ | √ | | √ | | √ | |
| Roots and radicals | | | | | | | | | | | | | √ | | √ | | | √ | √ | √ | | | | | | | | √ | | | | | √ | | | |
| Fractions: read, write, compare, order | | | | | √ | | √ | | | | | | | | | | | | | | | | √ | | √ | | | | | | | | | | | |
| Fractions: rounding | | | | | | | | √ | | | | | | √ | | | | | | | | | | | | | | | | | | | | | | |
| Equivalent fractions | | | | | | | | √ | | | | | | | | | | √ | | | | √ | √ | | | √ | | | | | | | | | | |
| Fractions in lowest terms | | | | | | | | | √ | | | | | | | √ | √ | | | | | | | | | | | √ | | | | | √ | | | |
| Ratios | | | | | | | | | √ | | | | | | | √ | | | | | | √ | | | | | | | | | | | √ | | | |
| Proportions | | | | | | | | | | | √ | | | | √ | | | | | | | | | | | | | √ | | | | | | | | √ |
| Decimals: read, write, compare, order | | | | | | √ | | | | | | √ | | | | | | √ | | | | | | | √ | √ | | | | | | | √ | | √ | |
| Decimals: rounding | | | | | | | | | | | | | | | | | | | | | | | | | | | √ | | | | | | | | | |
| Percent | | | | | | | | | √ | | | | | | | | | | | | | | √ | | | | | √ | | | | | √ | | | |
| Fractions, decimals, percent relationships | | | | | | | | | | | | √ | | | | | | √ | | | | | | | | | | √ | | | | | | | | √ |
| Money | | | | | | | | | | √ | | | | | | | | | | √ | | | | | | | | | √ | | | | | | | |

Use It! Don't Lose It! IP 613-3

# INCENTIVE PUBLICATIONS DAILY PRACTICE SERIES
## GRADE 8 MATH SKILLS

### Operations/Computations

| Skill | 1 | 2 | 3 | 4 | 5 | 6 | 7 | 8 | 9 | 10 | 11 | 12 | 13 | 14 | 15 | 16 | 17 | 18 | 19 | 20 | 21 | 22 | 23 | 24 | 25 | 26 | 27 | 28 | 29 | 30 | 31 | 32 | 33 | 34 | 35 | 36 |
|---|---|---|---|---|---|---|---|---|---|---|---|---|---|---|---|---|---|---|---|---|---|---|---|---|---|---|---|---|---|---|---|---|---|---|---|---|
| Inverse operations | | √ | | | | | √ | | | | | | | | | | | | | | √ | | | | | | | | | √ | | | | √ | | |
| Properties | | √ | | √ | | | | √ | | | | | √ | | | √ | √ | | | | | √ | | | | √ | | | | √ | | | | | | |
| Order of operations | | | | √ | | | | | √ | | | | | √ | | | | √ | | | | | | √ | | √ | | | | | | | | | | |
| Add and subtract whole numbers | √ | √ | | | | | √ | | | | | | | | | | | √ | | | √ | √ | | | | | | √ | | | | | | | | |
| Multiply whole numbers | √ | | | | √ | | | | | | | | √ | | √ | | √ | | | √ | | | | √ | √ | | | | | | √ | √ | | | | √ |
| Divide whole numbers | | | | | | √ | | | √ | | | | | | √ | | | √ | | √ | √ | √ | | | | √ | | | | √ | | | √ | | √ | √ |
| Multiply and divide with multiples of 10 | | | | √ | | | | | √ | | √ | | | √ | | | | √ | | | √ | | √ | | | | | √ | | | | | √ | | | √ |
| Averages | | | √ | | | | | √ | | | | √ | | | √ | | | √ | | √ | | √ | | | | | √ | | √ | √ | | | | | √ | |
| Add and subtract fractions | √ | | | | | √ | | | | | | | | | | | | | | √ | | | √ | | | √ | | | | | √ | √ | | | | |
| Multiply fractions | | √ | | | √ | | | √ | √ | | √ | | √ | √ | √ | √ | √ | √ | | | √ | | | √ | | | √ | | | √ | | | √ | √ | | √ |
| Divide fractions | | | √ | √ | | | √ | | √ | √ | | | | | √ | | | √ | | | | | | √ | | | | | | | | | √ | √ | | |
| Add and subtract decimals | √ | √ | √ | | | | | | √ | | | | √ | | | | | √ | | √ | √ | | | √ | √ | | √ | | | | | √ | | √ | √ | |
| Multiply decimals | | √ | | | | √ | √ | | √ | | | | | | √ | | | | | √ | | √ | | | √ | | √ | | √ | | | | | √ | √ | √ |
| Divide decimals | | | | √ | | | | | | √ | | | | | √ | √ | √ | | | | | √ | | | | √ | | √ | | √ | | | √ | | | |
| Operations with money | | | | | √ | √ | √ | | √ | √ | | | | √ | √ | √ | | √ | | | | | √ | √ | | | | √ | | | √ | | √ | | | |
| Add integers | √ | | | √ | √ | | | | | | | √ | | √ | √ | √ | | | | | | | √ | √ | | | | | | √ | | | | | | |
| Subtract integers | √ | | | √ | | | | | | | √ | | | √ | | √ | √ | | | √ | | | √ | √ | | √ | √ | √ | | √ | | √ | √ | √ | √ | |
| Multiply integers | | √ | | | | √ | | | √ | | | | √ | | √ | √ | | | | | √ | | | √ | √ | | √ | | √ | | | √ | | | | √ |
| Divide integers | | | √ | | | | √ | | | | √ | √ | | | √ | √ | | √ | √ | | √ | | | | | | | | √ | | | | √ | | | |
| Compute with roots, radicals, or exponents | | | | | | | | | √ | | | | | | | √ | | | | | | √ | | √ | √ | | √ | √ | √ | √ | √ | √ | | | √ | |
| Estimate answers | | | √ | | | | | | | | | | | √ | | | | | | | | | | √ | √ | | | √ | √ | √ | | √ | | √ | √ | |
| Find missing operation | | | | | √ | | | | √ | | | | | | | √ | | | | | | | √ | √ | | √ | | | √ | √ | | | | | √ | √ |
| Verify accuracy of computations | | √ | √ | √ | | | √ | | | | | | | | √ | √ | √ | | | | | √ | | √ | √ | √ | | √ | √ | | | | | | | |

Use It! Don't Lose It! IP 613-3

# INCENTIVE PUBLICATIONS DAILY PRACTICE SERIES
## GRADE 8 MATH SKILLS

### Problem-Solving

| Skill | 1 | 2 | 3 | 4 | 5 | 6 | 7 | 8 | 9 | 10 | 11 | 12 | 13 | 14 | 15 | 16 | 17 | 18 | 19 | 20 | 21 | 22 | 23 | 24 | 25 | 26 | 27 | 28 | 29 | 30 | 31 | 32 | 33 | 34 | 35 | 36 |
|---|---|---|---|---|---|---|---|---|---|---|---|---|---|---|---|---|---|---|---|---|---|---|---|---|---|---|---|---|---|---|---|---|---|---|---|---|
| Identify problem | √ | | | | | | | | | | | | | | | | | | | | | | | | | | | | | | | | | | | |
| Necessary information | | √ | | | | √ | | | | | | | | | | | | | √ | | | | | | | | | | | √ | √ | | | | | √ |
| Necessary operations; order of operations | | | √ | √ | | | | √ | | √ | | | | | | | √ | | | | √ | √ | | | | | | | √ | | √ | √ | | | | |
| Choose or explain strategy | | | | √ | | | | | √ | | √ | | | | | √ | √ | | | | √ | √ | | | | | √ | √ | | | | | | | √ | |
| Translate into an equation | | | | | | | | | | | | √ | | | | √ | | √ | √ | | | √ | | | | | √ | | | √ | | | | | | |
| Extend a pattern | | | | √ | | √ | | | √ | | | | | | √ | | | | | √ | | | | | | | | √ | | | | | | | | |
| Use a formula | | | | | | | | √ | | √ | | √ | √ | √ | | | √ | | | √ | | √ | √ | √ | √ | √ | | | | | | | | | | |
| Use diagrams/illustrations | √ | | | | √ | √ | | | | | | | √ | √ | | | √ | | | | | | √ | √ | √ | | | | | | | | | | | |
| Use estimation | | √ | | | | | | √ | | √ | | √ | √ | | | | | | √ | √ | | | | | | √ | | | | | | | | √ | | |
| Use mental math | | | √ | | | | | | | | √ | | | √ | | | | | | | √ | | | | | | | | | √ | | | | | | |
| Use logic | | | | | | | | | | | | √ | | | | | | | | | | | | √ | | | | | | | | | √ | | | |
| Use trial and error | | | | √ | | | √ | | | | | | √ | | √ | | | √ | | | √ | | | | | | | √ | | √ | | | | | | |
| Use a graph or table | | | √ | | √ | | √ | | | | | | √ | | | | | √ | √ | | √ | √ | | √ | √ | √ | | | √ | | | | √ | √ | √ | |
| Set up a proportion | | | √ | | | | | | √ | | | | | | | √ | | | √ | √ | | | | | | | √ | | √ | | | | | | | |
| Problems w/ whole numbers | √ | | | | | | | √ | | √ | | | | | | | | | | | | | | | | | √ | | √ | | | √ | | | | |
| Problems w/ fractions | | | | √ | | | | | √ | | | | | | | | | √ | | | | √ | √ | | | √ | √ | √ | | | | | | | | |
| Problems w/ decimals | | √ | | | √ | | √ | | | | | | √ | | | √ | | | | | √ | √ | √ | √ | | | √ | √ | | | | | | | | |
| Problems w/ percent | | | | √ | | | | | | √ | √ | | | | √ | | √ | | | √ | √ | | | √ | √ | | √ | √ | | | | | √ | | | |
| Problems w/ roots, radicals, or exponents | | | | | | | | | | | | | | | | | | | | √ | | | | | | | | √ | | √ | | | | | | |
| Problems w/ positive and negative numbers | | | | | | √ | √ | | | √ | | | √ | | | | √ | √ | √ | | | √ | | | | | | √ | | | | | √ | | | |
| Problems w/ rate or ratio | √ | | | √ | | | | | | | | | √ | | √ | | √ | | √ | √ | √ | √ | | √ | | | √ | | | | | | √ | √ | | |
| Problems w/ money | | | | | √ | | | | | | | | | | | √ | | | | | | √ | | | | √ | | | √ | | | | | | | |
| Problems w/ time | | | | | | | | √ | | √ | | | | | | | | | | | | | | | √ | | √ | √ | | | √ | | | | √ | |
| Problems w/ measurement | | | | | | | | √ | | √ | | √ | √ | | √ | | | | √ | | | | | √ | √ | | √ | √ | √ | √ | √ | | | √ | | |
| Problems w/statistics | | | | | | √ | | | | | √ | | | | | | | | | | | √ | | | | | | √ | √ | | | | √ | | | |
| Problems w/probability | | | | | √ | | | | | √ | | | | | | √ | | | | | | √ | | | | | | | | | | √ | | √ | | |
| Open-ended problems | | | | | | | | | | | | | | | √ | | √ | | √ | | | | | | √ | | | | | | | √ | | | | |
| Reasonableness or accuracy of solutions | | | √ | | | √ | | | √ | | | √ | | √ | | | | | | | | | √ | | | | √ | | | | | √ | | | | |

© Incentive Publications, Inc., Nashville, TN

Use It! Don't Lose It! IP 613-3

# INCENTIVE PUBLICATIONS DAILY PRACTICE SERIES
## GRADE 8 MATH SKILLS

### Geometry

| Skill | 1 | 2 | 3 | 4 | 5 | 6 | 7 | 8 | 9 | 10 | 11 | 12 | 13 | 14 | 15 | 16 | 17 | 18 | 19 | 20 | 21 | 22 | 23 | 24 | 25 | 26 | 27 | 28 | 29 | 30 | 31 | 32 | 33 | 34 | 35 | 36 |
|---|---|---|---|---|---|---|---|---|---|---|---|---|---|---|---|---|---|---|---|---|---|---|---|---|---|---|---|---|---|---|---|---|---|---|---|---|
| Points, lines, line segments, rays, and planes | √ | | | | | | | | | | | | | | | | | | | | | | | | | | | | | | | | | | | |
| Angles | √ | √ | | | | | √ | √ | | √ | | | √ | | √ | | √ | √ | √ | √ | √ | | √ | | | √ | √ | √ | | | | √ | √ | √ | | √ |
| Identify plane figures | | √ | | | | | | | √ | | | | | | √ | | √ | | | √ | √ | | | | | √ | √ | | | | | | | | | |
| Properties of plane figures | | | √ | | √ | | √ | | | | | √ | | √ | | | | | | | | | | | √ | | | | | | | | √ | | √ | |
| Symmetry | | | √ | | | | | | | | | | | | | √ | | | | | | | | | √ | | | | | | | | | √ | | |
| Transformations | | | | √ | | | | | | √ | | | | | | | √ | | | | | | | | | √ | | | | | | | | | | |
| Identify space figures | | | | | | | | √ | | | | √ | | √ | √ | | | √ | | √ | | √ | √ | | | | | | √ | | √ | | | | | |
| Properties of space figures | | | | | √ | | | | √ | | √ | | | | √ | | | | √ | √ | √ | | | | √ | | | √ | | √ | | | | | | √ |
| Similar figures | | | | | √ | | | | | | | | √ | | | | | | | | | | | √ | | | | | | | | | | √ | | |
| Congruent figures | | | | | | √ | | | | | | | | | √ | | √ | | | | √ | | | | | | √ | | √ | | | | | | √ | |
| Draw figures | | | | | | √ | | | √ | √ | | | | | √ | | | | | √ | √ | | | | | | | | √ | | | | | | √ | √ |

### Measurement

| Skill | 1 | 2 | 3 | 4 | 5 | 6 | 7 | 8 | 9 | 10 | 11 | 12 | 13 | 14 | 15 | 16 | 17 | 18 | 19 | 20 | 21 | 22 | 23 | 24 | 25 | 26 | 27 | 28 | 29 | 30 | 31 | 32 | 33 | 34 | 35 | 36 |
|---|---|---|---|---|---|---|---|---|---|---|---|---|---|---|---|---|---|---|---|---|---|---|---|---|---|---|---|---|---|---|---|---|---|---|---|---|
| Measurement units | √ | √ | | | | | | | √ | | | | | | | | | | √ | | | | | | | √ | √ | | | √ | | | √ | | | |
| Estimate measurements | | | √ | | | | | | | | | | | | √ | | | √ | | | | | | √ | √ | | | | √ | | | | | √ | | √ |
| Convert units | | | √ | √ | | | | | √ | | | | | √ | | | √ | | √ | √ | | | | | | | | | √ | | | | | √ | | √ |
| Angle measurements | | | √ | | | | √ | | | √ | | | | | | | | | | √ | | √ | √ | | √ | √ | | | | √ | | | | | √ | |
| Measure length | √ | | | | | | √ | | | | | | | | | | | | | | | | | | | | | | | | | | | | | |
| Choose correct formula | | | | | | | | √ | √ | | | √ | | √ | | | √ | | | √ | | | √ | | | √ | √ | | √ | | | | | | | |
| Perimeter, circumference | | | √ | √ | | | | | √ | | | √ | | √ | | | | | √ | √ | | | | | | | | | | | | | | | | |
| Area of plane figures | | | | √ | √ | √ | | | | | | √ | | √ | | | | | | | | | | | √ | | √ | | √ | | | | | √ | | √ |
| Surface area (space figures) | | | | | | | | √ | | | | | | | | √ | | | | | | | | | | | | √ | | | | | | | | √ |
| Volume of space figures | | | | √ | | | | | √ | √ | | √ | | | | √ | √ | | | √ | √ | | | √ | √ | | | | √ | | | | | √ | | |
| Temperature | | | | | | √ | | | | | | | | | √ | | | | | | √ | √ | √ | | | | | | | | | | | | | |
| Time | | | | | | | | | | √ | | √ | | | | | | | | √ | | | | | | | | √ | | √ | | | √ | | | |
| Weight | | | | √ | √ | | | | | | | | | | | | | | | √ | | | | | √ | | | | | | √ | | | | | |
| Scale | | | | | √ | | | | | | | | | | | | | | | | | | | √ | √ | | | | √ | | | | | | | |
| Reasonableness of a measurement | | | | | | | | √ | | | | | | | | | | √ | | | | √ | | | | | | | √ | | | | | | √ | |
| Compare measurements | | | | √ | | | | | | | √ | √ | | | | √ | | | | | | | | | | √ | | | √ | | √ | √ | | √ | | √ |

Use It! Don't Lose It! IP 613-3

# INCENTIVE PUBLICATIONS DAILY PRACTICE SERIES
## GRADE 8 MATH SKILLS

## Statistics & Graphing

| Skill | 1 | 2 | 3 | 4 | 5 | 6 | 7 | 8 | 9 | 10 | 11 | 12 | 13 | 14 | 15 | 16 | 17 | 18 | 19 | 20 | 21 | 22 | 23 | 24 | 25 | 26 | 27 | 28 | 29 | 30 | 31 | 32 | 33 | 34 | 35 | 36 |
|---|---|---|---|---|---|---|---|---|---|---|---|---|---|---|---|---|---|---|---|---|---|---|---|---|---|---|---|---|---|---|---|---|---|---|---|---|
| Define statistical terms | √ | | | | | | | | | | | | | √ | | | | | | | | | | | | | | | | | | | | | | |
| Interpret tables | √ | | | | √ | | | √ | | | | | | | √ | | | | | | | √ | √ | | | | | | | | √ | √ | | | | |
| Find mean, range, median, mode in a set of data | | | | √ | | | | | √ | | | | | | | √ | | | | | | | | √ | √ | | √ | √ | | √ | | | | √ | | |
| Select appropriate graph | | | √ | | | | | | | | √ | | | | | | √ | | | | | | | | | √ | | | | | | | | | √ | |
| Interpret graphs | | √ | | √ | | | | | | | √ | | √ | | | | | √ | √ | | √ | √ | | | | | | | | | | | | | | |
| Solve problems from data | | | | | | √ | | | √ | | √ | | √ | √ | | | | | √ | | √ | | √ | | √ | | √ | | | √ | | √ | | | | √ |
| Translate data into a graph or table | | | | | √ | | | | | | | | | | | √ | | | | | | | | √ | | | | | | | | | √ | | | |
| Coordinate graphs | | | | | | | √ | | | | | | | | | | | | | | | | | | | | | | √ | | | | | | | |

## Probability

| Skill | 1 | 2 | 3 | 4 | 5 | 6 | 7 | 8 | 9 | 10 | 11 | 12 | 13 | 14 | 15 | 16 | 17 | 18 | 19 | 20 | 21 | 22 | 23 | 24 | 25 | 26 | 27 | 28 | 29 | 30 | 31 | 32 | 33 | 34 | 35 | 36 |
|---|---|---|---|---|---|---|---|---|---|---|---|---|---|---|---|---|---|---|---|---|---|---|---|---|---|---|---|---|---|---|---|---|---|---|---|---|
| Define probability terms | | √ | | | | | √ | | | | | | | | | | | | | | | | | | | | | | | | | | | | | |
| Describe likelihood of an event | √ | | | | | | | | | | | | | | | | | | | | √ | | | | | | | | | | | | | | | √ |
| Outcomes of one event | | | √ | | | | | | | | | | | | | | | | | | | | | | √ | | | | | | | | | | | |
| Probability of one event | | | | √ | | | | | √ | | | √ | | √ | | √ | | | | √ | | | | √ | | | | | | | | | | | √ | |
| Outcomes of two independent events | | | | | √ | | | | | | | | | | √ | | | | | | | | √ | | | | | | | | | | | | | |
| Tree diagrams | | | | | | √ | | | | | | | | | | | | | | | | | | | | | | | | √ | | | | | | |
| Probability of two independent events | | | | | | √ | √ | | | | √ | | | | | | | | | | | √ | | | | | | | | | | √ | | √ | | |
| Outcomes/probability of two dependent events | | | | | | | | √ | | | | | | | | | | √ | | | | | √ | | | | √ | | | | √ | | √ | | | |
| Combinations and permutations | | | | | | | | | | | | | | | | | | | √ | | | | | | | √ | √ | | | | √ | | | | | |
| Odds for or against | | | | | | | | | | √ | | | | | | | | | | √ | | | | | | | | | √ | | | | | | | √ |
| Random sampling | | | | | | | | | | | | | √ | | | | | | | | √ | | | | | | | √ | | | | √ | | | | |

117

Use It! Don't Lose It! IP 613-3

# INCENTIVE PUBLICATIONS DAILY PRACTICE SERIES
## GRADE 8 MATH SKILLS

*Pre-Algebra*

| Skill | 1 | 2 | 3 | 4 | 5 | 6 | 7 | 8 | 9 | 10 | 11 | 12 | 13 | 14 | 15 | 16 | 17 | 18 | 19 | 20 | 21 | 22 | 23 | 24 | 25 | 26 | 27 | 28 | 29 | 30 | 31 | 32 | 33 | 34 | 35 | 36 |
|---|---|---|---|---|---|---|---|---|---|---|---|---|---|---|---|---|---|---|---|---|---|---|---|---|---|---|---|---|---|---|---|---|---|---|---|---|
| Identify characteristics of different numbers | √ | | | | | | | | | | | | | | | √ | | | | | | | | | | | | | | | | | | | | |
| Patterns and functions | √ | | | | | | | | | √ | | | | | √ | | | √ | | √ | √ | | √ | | | | | √ | √ | √ | | | | | √ | |
| Opposites; absolute value | √ | | | √ | | | √ | | | | | | | | | | | √ | | | √ | | | | | | | √ | | | | | | | | |
| Compute with positive and negative numbers | | √ | | √ | | | √ | | | √ | | | | | | | √ | | √ | | | | | | | √ | √ | | | √ | | | √ | | | √ |
| Identify terms, variables, and coefficients | | √ | | √ | | √ | | | √ | | | | | | √ | | | | | | | | √ | | | | | | | √ | | √ | | | √ | |
| Read and write expressions | √ | √ | √ | √ | | | | | | | √ | √ | | | | | √ | | | | √ | | | | | | | | | | √ | √ | | | | |
| Simplify expressions | | | | | √ | | | | | | | √ | √ | √ | | | √ | √ | | | | | | √ | | | | √ | | √ | √ | √ | | | | |
| Read, write, graph inequalities | | | | | | √ | | √ | | | √ | | | | √ | | | √ | √ | | √ | | √ | √ | | | √ | | | | √ | √ | | √ | | |
| Read and write equations | | | √ | | | √ | √ | | | | | √ | | √ | | | | √ | √ | | √ | √ | | | | √ | √ | √ | | | √ | | | √ | | |
| Match equations to problems | | | | | √ | | √ | √ | | | | | | √ | √ | | | √ | | | | | √ | | √ | √ | √ | √ | √ | | | | √ | √ | √ | √ |
| Simplify equations | | | | | | √ | √ | √ | √ | √ | √ | √ | √ | √ | √ | | | | √ | √ | √ | | √ | √ | √ | | √ | | | | | | √ | √ | √ | √ |
| Solve equations – one variable, one step | | | | | | | √ | √ | √ | | | √ | | | | | | | √ | | | | √ | | | | | | | | | | | | | |
| Solve equations – one variable, multiple steps | | | | | | | | √ | √ | √ | | | | √ | √ | | | √ | √ | √ | √ | | | √ | | √ | √ | √ | √ | √ | √ | √ | √ | √ | √ | √ |
| Solve equations with two variables; write solution sets | | | | | | | | | | √ | | √ | | √ | √ | | | | | √ | √ | √ | | | √ | √ | | | | √ | √ | √ | | | √ | √ |
| Graphs of linear equations | | | | | | | | | √ | | | | √ | | | | | | | | | | | | √ | | | | √ | √ | | | | √ | | |
| Order of operations in equations | | | | | | | | | | √ | | | | | | | √ | | | | | | √ | | | | | | | | | | | | √ | |
| Verify accuracy of solutions | | | | | | | | √ | | | | | √ | | | | | | | | √ | | | | | | | | | | | √ | √ | | | |

118

Use It! Don't Lose It! IP 613-3

## Week 1 (pages 5–7)

**MONDAY**
1. b
2. no
3. 200, 175
4. range
5. C & F

**TUESDAY**
1. A
2. 400,404
3. 90.133
4. pints, inches, miles, quarts, ounces
5. Half of the players forgot to wash their uniforms. Charlie is 6 feet, 2 inches tall.

**WEDNESDAY**
1. multiplication
2. obtuse
3. −55.7
4. 5
5. 2004

**THURSDAY**
1. |50|
2. $\frac{11}{12}$
3. 3,003; 3,033; 3,333; 30,303; 33,033
4. 8 liters
5. 8.5 cm; $3\frac{1}{2}$ in.

**FRIDAY**
1. −82
2. 24,300
3. c
4. d
5. 20 backslaps

## Week 2 (pages 8–10)

**MONDAY**
1. c
2. 9,157
3. b
4. 24,882 shells
5. D and F

**TUESDAY**
1. 90,000
2. 4
3. 4.32
4. meters
5. addition and multiplication. Add, then multiply, then add.

**WEDNESDAY**
1. 12.84 m
2. trapezoid
3. n
4. −840
5. private donations

**THURSDAY**
1. −7.5
2. $\frac{3}{5}$
3. Estimates will vary. Somewhere around 270 – 280 $in^3$
4. 49,900
5. c

**FRIDAY**
1. $\frac{3}{12}$ or $\frac{1}{4}$
2. a
3. −30
4. 21 min.
5. 24 (Crab will pass 500 feet total on the 24th trip after the first 6.)

## Week 3 (pages 11–13)

**MONDAY**
1. 8,084 ÷ 94 = 86 OR 8,084 ÷ 86 = 94
2. a
3. 70 – 3x
4. 1, 2, 3, 4, 5, or 6
5. A. 360 grams
   B. 11 grams per second

**TUESDAY**
1. 45.741
2. 9, 51, 30, 80
3. −7
4. none
5. one

**WEDNESDAY**
1. b
2. yes
3. 8
4. a
5. c and d

**THURSDAY**
1. five times the difference between a number and twelve
2. $\frac{9}{16}$
3. 90,000
4. 15, 30, 45, 60
5. $\frac{120}{38,000} = \frac{x}{2,000}$ OR $\frac{38,000}{120} = \frac{2,000}{x}$

**FRIDAY**
1. 1,270 or 1,300
2. 55
3. 1, 2, 4, 7, 14, 28
4. d
5. no

## Week 4 (pages 14–16)

**MONDAY**
1. 7,600,000
2. 25 mph
3. −5
4. b
5. 2 days

**TUESDAY**
1. 7.6
2. a
3. $5x^2$ and $3x^2$
4. false
5. 11 hours

**WEDNESDAY**
1. −28
2. 34
3. 58
4. C
5. $\frac{2}{6}$ or $\frac{1}{3}$

**THURSDAY**
1. 235 on-time trips
2. $\frac{x^2}{4y}$ or $x^2 \div 4y$
3. 729
4. $\frac{3}{5} + \frac{7}{9}$
5. the circumference of the circle

**FRIDAY**
1. yes
2. add
3. 6d + 5
4. 330 $m^2$
5. Charlie's pattern: add 3 each month to previous month number; September: 26, October: 29, November: 32, December: 35
   Max's pattern: First month, add 1; From then on, add 1 more each month to his number for the previous month (i.e: Feb, add 2; Mar, add 3, and so on). September: 36, October: 45, November: 55, December: 66.

## Week 5 (pages 17–19)

**MONDAY**
1. 260
2. 4
3. 8a + 5b + 12
4. isosceles or equilateral
5. Runaway Train

**TUESDAY**
1. $\frac{5}{4}$
2. $582.48
3. six million, sixty thousand, six hundred six
4. 200.96 $in^2$
5. $\frac{1}{4}(x + 3x) = /$

**WEDNESDAY**
1. Answers will vary. Two possibilities are: 2 quarters, 2 dimes, and 6 pennies OR 6 dimes, 3 nickels, and 1 penny.

# ANSWER KEY

2. –5(n + 14)
3. 40
4. H,1; H,2; H,3; H,4; H,5; H,6; T,1; T,2; T,3; T,4; T,5; T,6
5. C, D

**THURSDAY**
1. c, d
2. $1\frac{8}{55}$
3. b (44.404)
4. –60, –30
5. yes

**FRIDAY**
1. 5 faces
2. c
3. multiply
4. 12 + 2x + (x – 4) = 95; x = 29
5. Examine graphs for accuracy

## Week 6 (pages 20–22)

**MONDAY**
1. 14 + 8p or 8p + 14
2. Problem: 2 – (–9) = 11 degrees
3. 26
4. A part of a line that has one endpoint and extends indefinitely in one direction.
5. Outcomes: 100,r; 100,y; 100,b; 50,r; 50,y; 50,b; 20,r; 20,y; 20,b

**TUESDAY**
1. >
2. Answers may vary. Some possibilities are: $\frac{3}{4}$, 75%, seventy-five hundredths, three quarters, seventy-five cents.
3. 88.451
4. 380 cm$^2$
5. the elevation change, the average age

**WEDNESDAY**
1. $\frac{\sqrt{n}}{4}$ = 39
2. –567
3. the frequency
4. no
5. D

**THURSDAY**
1. b, c, d
2. $\frac{20}{11}$
3. $8\frac{1}{2}$
4. 100° C
5. Tad, Chris, Alex

**FRIDAY**
1. 800 or 810
2. Events are dependent when the outcome of one event is affected by the outcome of a previous event.

3. 33
4. x = 9, –9
5. Kris

## Week 7 (pages 23–25)

**MONDAY**
1. a
2. 15d – 12 = 33
3. 7,812 ÷ 42 = 186 OR 7,812 ÷ 186 = 42
4. 9.682 minutes
5. (2,2); (3,7); (4,5); (6,4); (0,4); (–5, 0); (–4, 3); (–3,5); (–4,6); (–6,8)

**TUESDAY**
1. 80.08; 88.1488; 88.184; 88.1848
2. irrational
3. 9.96
4. 6 cm
5. 13 times

**WEDNESDAY**
1. –905
2. 90, 180
3. x = 88
4. 3 – (–47.5) = 50.5 ft
5. $\frac{6}{16}$ or $\frac{3}{8}$

**THURSDAY**
1. $\frac{5}{8}$; $\frac{2}{3}$; $\frac{5}{7}$; $\frac{3}{4}$
2. 9 fish
3. $1\frac{1}{24}$
4. 55m$^2$
5. no

**FRIDAY**
1. no, should be 3,278
2. The **odds in favor** is the numerical chance that an outcome will happen in comparison to another likelihood (or, the ratio of favorable outcomes to unfavorable outcomes). The statement is NOT true.
3. –742.55
4. $1316.75
5. Joe is 12.

## Week 8 (pages 26–28)

**MONDAY**
1. $\frac{3}{7}$
2. b + b$^2$ = 4
3. 638 miles
4. 37°
5. 1,933

**TUESDAY**
1. 1
2. 2,400 cm$^2$
3. x = 7.5
4. 700

5. 10:20 A.M. on Monday

**WEDNESDAY**
1. 8 hours
2. –49
3. >
4. Answers will vary.
5. #265, Tampa

**THURSDAY**
1. $\frac{3}{10}$
2. no
3. $\frac{100}{120}$ and $\frac{75}{90}$
4. no, y = –1000
5. Answer is 140 passengers. There are several ways to find the answer. Two possible ways are outlined here. *Method 1:* Divide (168 by 6); divide by 2 (or multiply by $\frac{1}{2}$); multiply (14 by 6); multiply (14 by 4); add (84 and 56) *Method 2:* Divide (168 by 6); divide by 2 (or multiply by $\frac{1}{2}$); multiply (14 by 2); subtract (28 from 168)

**FRIDAY**
1. no correct solutions
2. distributive property of multiplication
3. 3.91 x 10$^8$
4. –141.1
5. No, she can get only 48 boxes into the suitcase.

## Week 9 (pages 29–31)

**MONDAY**
1. p = – 5
2. $\frac{5}{8}$
3. multiply the exponential number
4. 12 edges
5. Strategies may vary. A likely strategy is to change elements to a common element for the calculations. Answer: 538.5 minutes OR 8 hours, 58.5 minutes

**TUESDAY**
1. $\frac{7}{9}$; $\frac{19}{21}$
2. two
3. 10.2639
4. 1000 in$^3$
5. yes

**WEDNESDAY**
1. c
2. yes
3. 2,450
4. 12 seconds
5. Answers will vary. Check student drawings.

**THURSDAY**
1. 1, 2, 3, 4, 6, 12 (12)
2. divide (÷)
3. oz, L, mL, C, or pt
4. $y = n^{10}$
5. 2002

**FRIDAY**
1. 45,000
2. a, b, c, e
3. 1200
4.         38n – 66 = 86
    38n – 66 + 66 = 86 + 66
*(Add 66 to both sides)*
    38n ÷ 38 = 152 ÷ 38
*(Divide both sides by 38.)*
           n = 4
5. The next 4 figures in the pattern are:

## Week 10 (pages 32–34)

**MONDAY**
1. 74,929
2. y = 250
3. the number that falls in the middle, when all the numbers are written in order from least to greatest
4. Answers will vary. Check to see that student drawing is a slide of the figure (no flip or turn).
5. First add 163 and 73, then subtract (1526 – 236). Answer is 1,290 feet.

**TUESDAY**
1. $\frac{12}{18}$ OR $\frac{2}{3}$
2. 1188.88
3. $V = \pi r^2 \times h$
4. a (5100 k)
5. Wed day 80; Th night 63;
Fri day 93; Sat night 78

**WEDNESDAY**
1. six
2. –6882
3. false (a chord does not have to pass through the center)
4. $15 + 5w^2 = 35$
5. $1\frac{1}{2}$ C cactus chunks
  $2\frac{2}{3}$ C crushed tumbleweed
  $3\frac{1}{4}$ C cactus juice
  4 lizard eggs
  $2\frac{1}{4}$ T crumbled flower petals
  $3\frac{1}{3}$ qt water

**THURSDAY**
1. Multiply 7 times b and 7 times 9.

2. $57.88
3. $\frac{2}{3}$
4. 6.4%
5. 38.475 $ft^3$

**FRIDAY**
1. 560.4, OR $560\frac{4}{10}$
2. y = –24
3. 2504.26
4. F
5. 7:55 A.M.; 1:08 P.M. lunch stop

## Week 11 (pages 35–37)

**MONDAY**
1. 75% of the competitions
2. 101
3. six
4. the sum of thirty and nine times the difference between a number cubed and seven
5. a, b, c, f

**TUESDAY**
1. yes
2. 3.85
3. $b^2 = 144$
4. 3925 $in^3$
5. a. 196 in favor
   b. 140 kids

**WEDNESDAY**
1. – 54
2. x = 15
3. $\frac{30}{36}$ or $\frac{5}{6}$
4. two faces
5. head injuries

**THURSDAY**
1. x = 420
2. $1\frac{41}{63}$
3. 900°
4. =
5. Answers will vary; here are some possibilities: 1,250, 1,232, 1,340, 1,052

**FRIDAY**
1. a, d
2. no
3. z = 92
4. $150.00 to $160.00
5. no; strategies will vary

## Week 12 (pages 38–40)

**MONDAY**
1. $\frac{8}{15}$
2. 3x = 129
3. scattergram
4. true
5. 810 times

**TUESDAY**
1. 4500 or 5000 meters
2. 80,634
3. Twice the cube of a number divided by five is less than sixty.
4. 48
5. sphere

**WEDNESDAY**
1. 662
2. $r = \frac{d}{t}$ (Answer is r = 54.4 mph.)
3. cube or rectangular prism
4. $\frac{35}{1}$
5. 1$^{st}$ place: Angela, green suit;
2$^{nd}$ place: Ralph, red suit;
3$^{rd}$ place: Gabe, blue suit

**THURSDAY**
1. $9\frac{8}{15}$
2. 24
3. 7n – 91
4. x + 2x + (2x + 46) = 246;
(Kurt's time = 2x + 46 = 126 hours)
5. A. 99 years, 61 days;
B. Answers will vary.

**FRIDAY**
1. multiplication
2. 42
3. $\frac{2}{4}$ or $\frac{1}{2}$
4. Missing numbers top to bottom
  y = 4 (–2, 4)
  x = –1 (–1, 2)
  y = 0 (0, 0)
  x = 2 (2, –4)
  y = –6 (3, –6)
5. Check grids to see that drawings are placed at correct points.

## Week 13 (pages 41–43)

**MONDAY**
1. 356,400
2. $\frac{294\,ft^2}{hour}$
3. x = 30
4. d, f
5. Tara

**TUESDAY**
1. yes
2. Equation: $\frac{74}{30} = \frac{x}{120}$
(Or, $\frac{74}{.5} = \frac{x}{2}$)
Solution = 296 weeds
3. 50,555,000; 50,550,050;
50,550,005
4. 130 ft
5. 12 bags

**WEDNESDAY**
1. $4b^5 + 12$
2. 386 handfuls

# ANSWER KEY

3. –389,200
4. 5,700 beetles
5. CD is parallel to YZ;
   EF is parallel to WX

### THURSDAY
1. 6
2. $\frac{3}{4}$
3. g = –7
4. 163.2 cm$^3$
5. yes

### FRIDAY
1. Yes, it is one of two possible solutions.
2. 1.6; 160%
3. distributive
4. 41,976 + 56,789 = 98,765 OR 56,789 + 41,976 = 98,765
5. Brad

## Week 14 (pages 44–46)

### MONDAY
1. 10,102
2. Data is numerical information
3. Equation: x + (x – 103) = 217; Answer is 160 sec or 2 min, 40 sec.
4. Possible characteristics are: 4 equal sides, 4 right angles, 2 sets of parallel sides, 4 sides
5. worms

### TUESDAY
1. $412.56
2. q = 36.5
3. 45.2 beans/minute
4. 1,750,000
5. A = $\frac{1}{2}$h(b$_1$ + b$_2$); A = 120m$^2$

### WEDNESDAY
1. –144
2. pyramid with a triangular base
3. $\frac{21}{26}$
4. 12a
5. approx 21 ft$^3$

### THURSDAY
1. 54 grapes
2. 1$\frac{5}{6}$
3. 700,070,070
4. 11,024
5. Check graphs for accuracy.

### FRIDAY
1. 18,000,000
2. d
3. a. b = 40

b. b = 43
4. the division inside the parentheses 9,000 ÷ 25
5. a. 2001
   b. 1998
   c. MCCIX
   d. MDCCCXXX
   e. MDCCCXCV

## Week 15 (pages 47–49)

### MONDAY
1. yes
2. 456, R 100
3. 7
4. Check to see that figures are similar.
5. P8 = $\frac{3}{8}$; P not 6 = $\frac{6}{8}$ or $\frac{3}{4}$; P not 6 and not 8 = $\frac{3}{8}$

### TUESDAY
1. 628 ft
2. 3024, 720
3. 5k = –50
4. 8.5
5. 35 rows of seats

### WEDNESDAY
1. –87
2. 141.67 lbs.
3. 13, 7, 0, 5
4. Check to see that students have drawn trapezoids.
5. 73 tricks

### THURSDAY
1. >
2. no
3. 28°C
4. $\frac{25}{33}$
5. 50,000 shows

### FRIDAY
1. 1200
2. 8$^7$ x 10$^3$
3. x = –4
4. A and C; B and D
5. Check student drawings. The pattern is in the number of flags. The pattern to this point is 1, 1, 0, 2, 2, 0, 3, 3, 0, 4. So the next tent would have 4 flags; the next would have 0 flags; and the 3$^{rd}$ would have 5 flags.

## Week 16 (pages 50–52)

### MONDAY
1. 782,210
2. 31,560 pages
3. 6x = 12
4. 6 different combinations
5. A, (five), C (eight), D (eight), E (one)

### TUESDAY
1. Equation: $\frac{3}{24} = \frac{12}{x}$ (or $\frac{24}{3} = \frac{x}{12}$)
   Solution: 96 visits
2. s = –17
3. 27 medals
4. 5.51
5. B (cylinder) has greater volume; A (prism) has greater surface area

### WEDNESDAY
1. –179
2. the sum of six times the square of a number, twice that number, and four
3. 1.6 to 210
4. no
5. 108.69 pushups per minute Explanations will vary.

### THURSDAY
1. a. $\frac{1}{3}$; b. 2$\frac{2}{5}$; c. $\frac{1}{20}$
2. 135 miles
3. n = 38
4. 1$\frac{1}{2}$
5. 188.7 kg

### FRIDAY
1. yes
2. the set of all positive or negative counting numbers and zero
3. 390
4. twelve possible outcomes: h & 1; h & 2; h & 3; h & 4; h & 5; h & 6; t & 1; t & 2; t & 3; t & 4; t & 5; t & 6
5. B (x = 39 feet)

## Week 17 (pages 53–55)

### MONDAY
1. 0
2. 18°
3. 50,000
4. $\frac{4}{24}$ or $\frac{1}{6}$
5. Strategies will vary. Answers are:
   A. 285.5
   B. 75.57

### TUESDAY
1. 25.5614 + 39.4706 = 65.032
2. x = 3.5 or 3$\frac{1}{2}$
3. d, e
4. V = 857$\frac{3}{8}$ in$^2$
5. his birth date

### WEDNESDAY
1. –88.3
2. Answers may vary—the best choices are a bar graph or a circle graph.
3. –11,520
4. 2 per month
5. slide and turn

**THURSDAY**
1. divide
2. $\frac{2}{3}$; $\frac{6}{9}$; $\frac{98}{147}$; $\frac{42}{63}$
3. $12^{4}{}_{5}$
4. 46.39°C
5. $\frac{49118}{169}$; 29,064 %

**FRIDAY**
1. d
2. multiply
3. $3y^2 - 2y$
4. the difference between the square root of two hundred fifty-six and seven times the sum of a number (s) and six
5. Examine student graphs to see that they are accurately constructed.

# Week 18 (pages 56–58)

**MONDAY**
1. hexagon
2. 7k = –132 (or –7k = 132)
3. 194,326
4. $699,078.97
5. approx $800 – $4,000

**TUESDAY**
1. 400
2. yes
3. no
4. $\frac{5}{11}$
5. no

**WEDNESDAY**
1. $\frac{2}{210}$ or $\frac{1}{105}$
2. 14,100
3. Answers will vary. One possibility: two $20s, two $10s, three $5s, two $1s
4. DBC (or CBD)
5. No answers are correct.

**THURSDAY**
1. Equation: –394 + x = 117; x = 511
2. $\frac{7}{10}$
3. quart, liter, gallon, pint, milliliter, cubic centimeter
4. <
5. Answers from top to bottom of table: y = 4 (–16, 4); x = –8 (–8, 2): y = 0 (0, 0); y = –2 (8, –2); x = 4 (4, –1)

**FRIDAY**
1. $84.51
2. yes
3. n = –30
4. add ($0.10 + $18.00)
5. Answers will vary.

# Week 19 (pages 59–61)

**MONDAY**
1. 120
2. 999
3. 3,281 ft
4. n = 188
5. JK

**TUESDAY**
1. feet
2. d = –.65
3. 12.07 k
4. 12.568
5. Conclusions may vary. Possibilities: The breaststroke is the slowest of the strokes. OR, The freestyle stroke gives the swimmer more speed than the other strokes shown.

**WEDNESDAY**
1. 73
2. pentagon
3. z = 11
4. yes
5. no

**THURSDAY**
1. 0.92
2.
3. 1
4. 7 records
5. 1157 m$^2$

**FRIDAY**
1. B
2. 60
3. 193
4. First and second digits in the answer are wrong; answer should be 1902.
5. A. laundry: 13,000
   B. bathroom: 17,000
   C. toilet: 17,000
   D kitchen: 8600

# Week 20 (pages 62–64)

**MONDAY**
1. all
2. h – 3(–4) = 48 or
   h = 48 + 3(–4)
   Solution: h = 60
3. 56,088
4. Check drawings.
5. $\frac{22}{18}$ or $1\frac{2}{9}$. Explanations will vary.

**TUESDAY**
1. –4g + 30
2. 2 pounds
3. 640.64

4. Al
5. V = Bh (B = area of base)
   V = 10,578 ft$^3$

**WEDNESDAY**
1. sampling
2. 22
3. Equation: $x + \frac{2}{3}x = 4,680$
   Solution: 2,808
4. 0
5. a. 31.5
   b. 189
   c. 115.5

**THURSDAY**
1. 3, 7, 23, 29, 47
2. $\frac{500}{3}$
3. $18\frac{1}{8}$
4. n = –6
5. 27,578.5 ft

**FRIDAY**
1. 85.5
2. p = 11, –11
3. 21,960,000
4. $\frac{6}{13}$
5. a. T
   b. F
   c. T
   d. T
   e. T
   f. F
   g. F
   h. F

# Week 21 (pages 65–67)

**MONDAY**
1. 1,111,111,110
2. $\frac{9}{3}$
3. the difference between a number (a) and twice the square of another number (b)
4. 8,000
5. Angle C

**TUESDAY**
1. 3,673,430,000
2. $16w^2 - 10w - 1470 = 0$
3. 211.112
4. A = 113.04 m$^2$
5. January 1, 1937

**WEDNESDAY**
1. $-40 + \frac{16}{n} \geq 4$
2. A central angle is formed by the intersection of two radii in a circle.
3. 20,400
4. Weight is between 1.8 lb and 2.6 lb.

# ANSWER KEY

5. Check graphs to see that points are accurately located.

## THURSDAY
1. Answers will vary depending on the year. Strategies will vary.
2. $57\frac{1}{5}$
3. $y = -4$
4. 660,016
5. 234.2 yd

## FRIDAY
1. The answer is correct; 4,236 x 20 = 86,520 or 20 x 4,326 = 86,520
2. a, b, c
3. 45,000
4. Independent events are events whose outcomes do not affect one another or are not dependent on one another; yes
5. kangaroo: 40 mph; cheetah: 62 mph; merganser: 50.6 mph; difference in rate: 11.4 mph

## Week 22 (pages 68–70)
### MONDAY
1. $-b -12 = \frac{(18 + 14)}{2}$
2. 54,721 R3
3. $2.93
4. 10
5. 7 hours

### TUESDAY
1. 6.65
2. 110 days
3. 6,000,000 + 300,000 + 900 + 20 + 5
4. –100.001
5. Equation: 8x + (x – 35) + (x – 18) = 996; Solution: 104.9 miles

### WEDNESDAY
1. subtract
2. Wed, Oct 26, at 5:00 pm (104 hours later); strategies will vary
3. –99
4. C
5. leapfrogging

### THURSDAY
1. $8^9$
2. $a = 3, -3$
3. $\frac{9}{16}$

4. no
5. Check student tables to see that they have created them in a way to help solve the problem. 27

## FRIDAY
1. Answers will vary, but should follow the format of x = x
2. Answers will vary. One possibility is y = 6, x = –3
3. 235, 468
4. $\frac{3}{14}$
5. 167 miles; Rates: treadmill: 4.8 mph; waterslide: 17.5 mph; bathtub: 3.8 mph; backward walk: 4 mph; wheelchair: 4.69 mph

## Week 23 (pages 71–73)
### MONDAY
1. 29.4 years
2. unlike
3. 2,707,000,000 or $2.707 \times 10^9$
4. sphere
5. Anne

### TUESDAY
1. $90\frac{13}{17}$
2. Understanding the pattern: to create each successive number, remove the last digit from the previous number and put it at the beginning of the number. Missing number is 3,480,167
3. 22.6802
4. 5917 $cm^3$
5. Divide 75 by 2; divide 37.5 by 9; add 15 to 60. Each bus weighs 4.17 metric tons.

### WEDNESDAY
1. –4,036
2. 108
3. 26y = 104
4. one 90° angle (right angle); and two angles less than 90° (acute angles)
5. no (Correct answer is 6.8)

### THURSDAY
1. 170
2. C = (F – 32) x $\frac{5}{9}$; $193\frac{1}{3}$°C
3. $\frac{1}{36}$
4. b = $\frac{-4000}{3}$
5. Two: F, H

### FRIDAY
1. $1.658 \times 10^9$ miles
2. 625
3. –2.11
4. First row of calculation should be

44,580. Second row should be moved to the left one place to account for multiplication by zero. Correct answer is 1,530,580.
5.  a. 76 pounds
    b. 180 pounds
    c. 76 pounds
    d. 540 pounds
    e. 240 pounds
    f. 186 pounds
    g. 300 pounds
    h. 6 pounds

## Week 24 (pages 74–76)
### MONDAY
1. 375 ft, 7.6 in
2. subtraction
3. $\frac{96}{240}$ or $\frac{2}{5}$
4. D, E
5. yes

### TUESDAY
1. ten millions place; ten thousands place; one thousands place; ones place
2. 550 cans
3. $96.50
4. a = –2.4
5. $74.55

### WEDNESDAY
1. –17
2. $20
3. < (Note: If x = 0 the two equations are equal.)
4. Check student drawings to make sure they have drawn cylinders; a, c, d
5.

### THURSDAY
1. 20p – 17q
2. 1 pound
3. 9
4. $34\frac{2}{5}$
5. V = $\frac{1}{3}\pi r^2 h$; c

### FRIDAY
1. c
2. divide
3. $\frac{3}{4}$d = 75
4. Answers will vary. Some possibilities: 250 x 40; 100 x 100; 200 x 50; 500 x 20; 25 x 400
5. Brad

## Week 25 (pages 77–79)

**MONDAY**
1. 10,425
2. 8,715 feet or 2,656 meters; must change to a common measurement unit—feet or meters
3. three times the difference between a number (n) and four
4. cylinder
5. 28,122 ft

**TUESDAY**
1. <
2. 0.933
3. $\frac{b}{5} + 3b^2$
4. 108 m$^2$
5. 36,000 in

**WEDNESDAY**
1. –28,800
2. $\frac{14}{35}$ or $\frac{2}{5}$
3. 850 ft
4. no
5. yes

**THURSDAY**
1. $\frac{3}{11}$ or $\frac{11}{3}$
2. $\frac{4}{35}$
3. full backpack
4. p = –12
5. November 20, 1938

**FRIDAY**
1. 50
2. 540°
3. 27,400
4. 24
5. 10,000 ft

## Week 26 (pages 80–82)

**MONDAY**
1. 3,000
2. 1929
3. 8
4. Check drawings to see that flip has been drawn.
5. b

**TUESDAY**
1. 36 flavors
2. 50.6
3. c = 12
4. Answers will vary. Some possibilities: $\frac{3}{5}$; $\frac{6}{10}$; $\frac{9}{15}$; $\frac{12}{20}$
5. b

**WEDNESDAY**
1. d = 60
2. 71m
3. –9

4. 35
5. a

**THURSDAY**
1. $146\frac{5}{9}$
2. protractor
3. six hundred sixteen ten thousandths
4. (5, 6); (–3, –10); (0, –4)
5. 4,300,000 patents

**FRIDAY**
1. Identity Property
2. 10t = 500
3. no; correct answer is 364,635
4. b
5. 13 triangles; 15 parallelograms; 18 trapezoids

## Week 27 (pages 83–85)

**MONDAY**
1. a bar graph
2. –2n = –20 or 20 = 2n
3. 8 pounds
4. Check to see that student has drawn a 6-sided, irregular figure
5. 375 lbs.

**TUESDAY**
1. 1.011111
2. 56.9%
3. 100.0325
4. Rule: Output is half of Input plus 1. Missing numbers from top to bottom: 6, 8, 3
5. d = 6.33 ft; C = 19.88 ft

**WEDNESDAY**
1. 2.4 ft$^3$/min
2. –73
3. 24
4. m = $19\frac{5}{9}$
5. a. line segment
   b. midpoint
   c. line
   d. perpendicular

**THURSDAY**
1. the milkshake
2. a. $\frac{3}{4}$   c. $22\frac{1}{3}$
   b. $\frac{1}{4}$   d. $\frac{3}{5}$
3. $\frac{2}{9}$
4.
5. 9,795 pasta eaters. Strategies will vary.

**FRIDAY**
1. multiply
2. 72.5 ft$^2$
3. f = –15
4. 58 in to 5980 in

5. a. 12.56 ft
   b. 16 slices
   c. 0.785 ft or 0.79 ft
   d. $6.25

## Week 28 (pages 86–88)

**MONDAY**
1. 9,629,568
2. $\frac{18}{6}$ or $\frac{3}{1}$
3. add
4. Dave
5. $\overline{JK}$

**TUESDAY**
1. $450 per point
2. 9.83 x 10$^{10}$
3. A number times the quotient of two hundred ten divided by seven is equal to six hundred.
4. 2,137 points
5. 9 ft

**WEDNESDAY**
1. 15 vertices
2. –7992
3. –9000
4. 38,387 points
5. 16 rebounds

**THURSDAY**
1. y = –7
2. Fraction: $\frac{216}{10,000}$; Decimal: 0.0216
3. $\frac{33}{35}$
4. 225°
5. Sunday 4:02 P.M; Strategies will differ.

**FRIDAY**
1. 18,600,000
2. 4x$^4$ + 48
3. –561
4. Proportion: $\frac{15}{9750} = \frac{x}{35,750}$; Solution: x = 55 games
5. blue: 3 pints; red: 2 pints; cost: $79.00

## Week 29 (pages 89–91)

**MONDAY**
1. 136.59 in$^2$
2. 1,177 participants
3. 54,544,545
4.
5. 4,020 Rudolph songs

**TUESDAY**
1. 52.544
2. $\frac{4}{7}$ or $\frac{20}{35}$
3. 101.6

# ANSWER KEY

4. 3,997 dimes
5. b

**WEDNESDAY**
1. In similar figures, the corresponding angles are equal. In congruent figures, the corresponding sides and angles are equal.
2. Multiply $\frac{2}{5}$ times 2,000,000.
3. b = 2
4. –6,981
5.

**THURSDAY**
1. 1,003,389
2. 8p + 3 = –17
3. $1\frac{7}{60}$
4. $70
5. B

**FRIDAY**
1. yes
2. divide by 10
3. 20 ft
4. yes
5. 1,028 m

## Week 30 (pages 92–94)

**MONDAY**
1. It is correct.
2. 108 million or 108,000,000 trees
3. k = 13
4. 115°
5. mode = 138 events;
   median = 208 events

**TUESDAY**
1. $a^3$, a, b
2. 136.4 – (–138.6) = 275°F
3. 2.55
4. 732, 904, 776, 5000
5. A. 192
   B. 300,000
   C. 25,200
   D. 792
   E. $\frac{1}{2}$
   F. 108
   G. $8\frac{1}{2}$
   H. 2
   I. 25,000
   J. 6
   K. 4,000
   L. 92,000

**WEDNESDAY**
1. 6.17 tornadoes
2. –100
3. g = –8.8
4. pyramid, triangle base
5. 1,b; 1,r; 1,g; 2,b; 2,r; 2,g; 3,b; 3,r; 3,g; 4,b; 4,r; 4,g;

**THURSDAY**
1. $\frac{1}{30}$
2. 35.2 mph
3. $7c^3 + 10c^2 + 10\,c - 31$
4. 12th of October
5. 94 miles

**FRIDAY**
1. no (Correct is $72,712.00)
2. no
3. 10,500,000
4. k = 97
5.

## Week 31 (pages 95–97)

**MONDAY**
1. the number of readers in North America
2. 88, R8
3. $\frac{26}{165}$
4. Answers will vary. Some possibilities: (3, 5); (6, 10); (12, 20)
5. a trapezoidal prism

**TUESDAY**
1. 34,200 m
2. –1200.45
3. 84
4. yes
5. 150 delivery persons

**WEDNESDAY**
1. –110
2. Answers will vary depending on today's date.
3. $32y^8 + 16y^2$
4. Check to see that triangles drawn have two equal angles.
5. Answers will vary. Possibilities: Circulation generally increased from 2000 to 2006, except for a decline in 2003 and 2004.
OR Circulation lagged in 2003 and 2004.
OR Overall, circulation increased from 2000 to 2006.

**THURSDAY**
1. $10\frac{2}{7}$
2. Multiply 1,094,000 by 6
3. no
4. a = 10 or –10
5. V = 753,600 $cm^3$

**FRIDAY**
1. subtract
2. 13 or 31
3. $203,005.00
4. 48n – 20 = 1,612 so n = 34
5. 20 (UBS, UBN, UBW, UBL, USN, USW, USL, UNW, UNL, UWL, BSN, BSW, BSL, BNW, BNL, BWL, SNW, SNL, SWL, NWL)

## Week 32 (pages 98–100)

**MONDAY**
1. 2,664,000
2. $2,493\frac{3}{5}$ ft
3. no
4. hexagonal prism; faces = 8; edges = 18; vertices = 12
5. two

**TUESDAY**
1. 59.493
2. 2:35 P.M., Oct. 19
3. $2x + 4y^2 + 135$
4. 8; 1; 17; 5; 31
5. no

**WEDNESDAY**
1. a. True; b. True
2. the sum of thirty times a number and one-half of another number
3. 12 different outcomes: RH, RT, PH, PT, BH, BT, GH, GT, YH, YT, GH, GT
4. –1650x + 21,450
5. divide; the difference in rate per hour is 1.53 mph

**THURSDAY**
1. $\frac{8}{17}$
2. 4
3. 835,279,100
4. the cube
5. 60 + x + 2x + (x + 35) = 395; x = 75 cards

**FRIDAY**
1. a
2. 200
3. x = 11; yes, x could also be –11
4. 2,280 people
5. 3 and 36; 4 and 27; 6 and 18; 9 and 12

## Week 33 (pages 101–103)

**MONDAY**
1. 40,000,000
2. $6.648 \times 10^7$
3. negative
4. octagon
5. $\frac{5}{51}$

**TUESDAY**
1. $700 = 35x$
2. $\frac{1}{15}$ ; $12\frac{1}{3}$ ; $\frac{1}{2}$
3. 26 lb, 11 oz
4. 100
5. 7 minutes

**WEDNESDAY**
1. $A = 45°$; $B = 90°$; $C = 45°$
2. –21
3. $n = 15$
4. 3.42 lb
5.

**THURSDAY**
1. $\frac{1}{10}$
2. Answers will vary
3. $1.552 \times 10^{14}$
4. 57.7355
5. a. sq ft, sq m, sq in, or sq cm
   b. ft, in, or cm
   c. in or cm
   d. degrees
   e. g, lb, or kg
   f. in, cm, ft, or m
   g. oz or g

**FRIDAY**
1. a
2. no ($k = 20$)
3. b (8,163,000)
4. 67,600
5. Anya

## Week 34 (pages 104–106)

**MONDAY**
1. 118,279
2. $\frac{8}{26}$ or $\frac{4}{13}$
3. $31x = 1$
4. five faces
5. 144 days

**TUESDAY**
1. 822.649
2. Answers will vary somewhat: about 30,500 feet
3. $c = 4$
4. $\frac{27}{324}$ or $\frac{1}{12}$

5. 87.92 m$^3$

**WEDNESDAY**
1. 65.5°
2. $\frac{6}{36}$ or $\frac{1}{6}$
3. d
4. no
5. yes

**THURSDAY**
1. 2
2. 113° and 67°
3. –30, –11, –15
4. yes
5. 76 years

**FRIDAY**
1. $(\frac{1}{2}c) + (\frac{1}{2} \times 90) + (\frac{1}{2} \times 8)$
2. no
3. $k - 66 = -44$
4. 67.5 ft$^2$
5. Check finished graphs to see that proportions are appropriate to numbers.

## Week 35 (pages 107–109)

**MONDAY**
1. 43 years, 131 days
2. 77
3. $\frac{10}{28}$ or $\frac{5}{14}$
4. Pattern: subtract 100 and add the next multiple of ten; 500
5. Check answers to see that students have finished the figure to create a complete symmetrical figure.

**TUESDAY**
1. 9.999
2. three
3. 1917
4. 12.2 in$^3$
5. (112 has least value. 55 has the greatest value.); difference is 3004

**WEDNESDAY**
1. 67,590
2. scattergram
3. $d = 5$
4. Answers will vary. Check to see that the figures drawn are identical to each other.
5. almost 6 years (5.99)

**THURSDAY**
1. $100\frac{1}{12}$
2. 31.6%
3. seven ten thousands and seven hundredths
4. multiply both sides by n
5. no

**FRIDAY**
1. 39 ft
2. b (200)
3. how many runs he scored during his career
4. no
5. $\frac{3}{8}$ ; $\frac{4}{7}$ ; $\frac{9}{13}$ ; $\frac{7}{10}$ ; $\frac{4}{5}$ ; $\frac{9}{11}$

## Week 36 (pages 110–112)

**MONDAY**
1. 989,901
2. 4,483,000
3. $\frac{5}{12}$
4. cylinder
5. a, b, e, f

**TUESDAY**
1. 2,500
2. 6 weeks
3. $q = -1700$
4. 126 cm$^2$
5. New York population: 8,008,278; Chicago population: 2,896,016; Philadelphia population: 1,517,550

**WEDNESDAY**
1. –21,300
2. a
3. $75b + 5a$
4. FBC (or CBF) and DBE (or EBD)
5. Tokyo's population

**THURSDAY**
1. 2%
2. $8\frac{15}{16}$
3. 3
4. Answers may vary somewhat. Student answers should be close to this: 82,217 vehicles
5. a. 0.044 m
   b. 1.3 L
   c. 50 cm
   d. 90 m
   e. 200,000 cm
   f. 0.33 kg
   g. 100 dm$^2$
   h. 30,000 mL

**FRIDAY**
1. multiply, subtract
2. 11.6 minutes
3. 600
4. no
5. a. Petronas Towers
   b. Aon Center
   c. China World Trade Center
   d. Jin Mao Building
   e. Tuntex 85 Sky Tower